A to Z 神秘案件

中英双语

第一辑

THE JAGUAR'S JEWEL

美洲豹宝石

[美]罗恩·罗伊 著
[美]约翰·史蒂文·格尼 绘 王芬芬 译

湖南少年儿童出版社
·长沙·

缅因州
加拿大
佛蒙特州
新罕布什尔州
纽约州
马萨诸塞州
绿地镇
康涅狄格州
纽约市
罗得岛州
宾夕法尼亚州
新泽西州
新泽西州
欢迎来到纽约市
一起解开
A to Z神秘案件
北
西
东
南

人物介绍

三人小组的成员，聪明勇敢，喜欢读推理小说，紧急关头总能保持头脑冷静。喜欢在做事之前好好思考！

丁丁

三人小组的成员，活泼机智，喜欢吃好吃的菜，常常有意想不到的点子。

乔希

三人小组的成员，活泼开朗，喜欢从头到脚穿同一种颜色的衣服，总是那个能找到大部分线索的人。

露丝

丁丁的伯伯，邀请丁丁和他的朋友来纽约玩。

沃伦·邓肯

和丈夫一起经营着纽约最好的法式餐厅。

伊冯娜

杰里米·皮茨

博士，珠宝鉴定家。

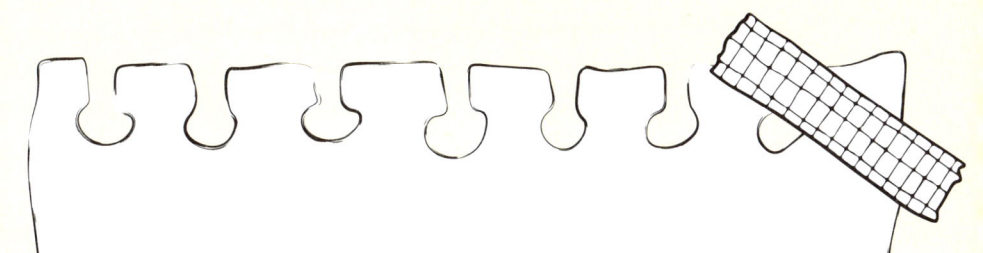

字母 J 代表 jackpot，头奖……

丁丁走近，用手指摸着条纹壁纸。在高于头顶的地方，他摸到了一条细小的缝。沿着细缝继续摸，他又摸到了另一条缝，这条缝一直延伸到地面。反方向两英尺的地方，还有第三条缝延伸到地面。这些缝几乎都藏在墙纸里面。

丁丁往后一跳，就像手被烧着了似的。"伙伴们！"他大声喊。

乔希和露丝跑进詹姆斯的办公室。

丁丁指引他们看缝隙。"我觉得这是一扇暗门！"他说。

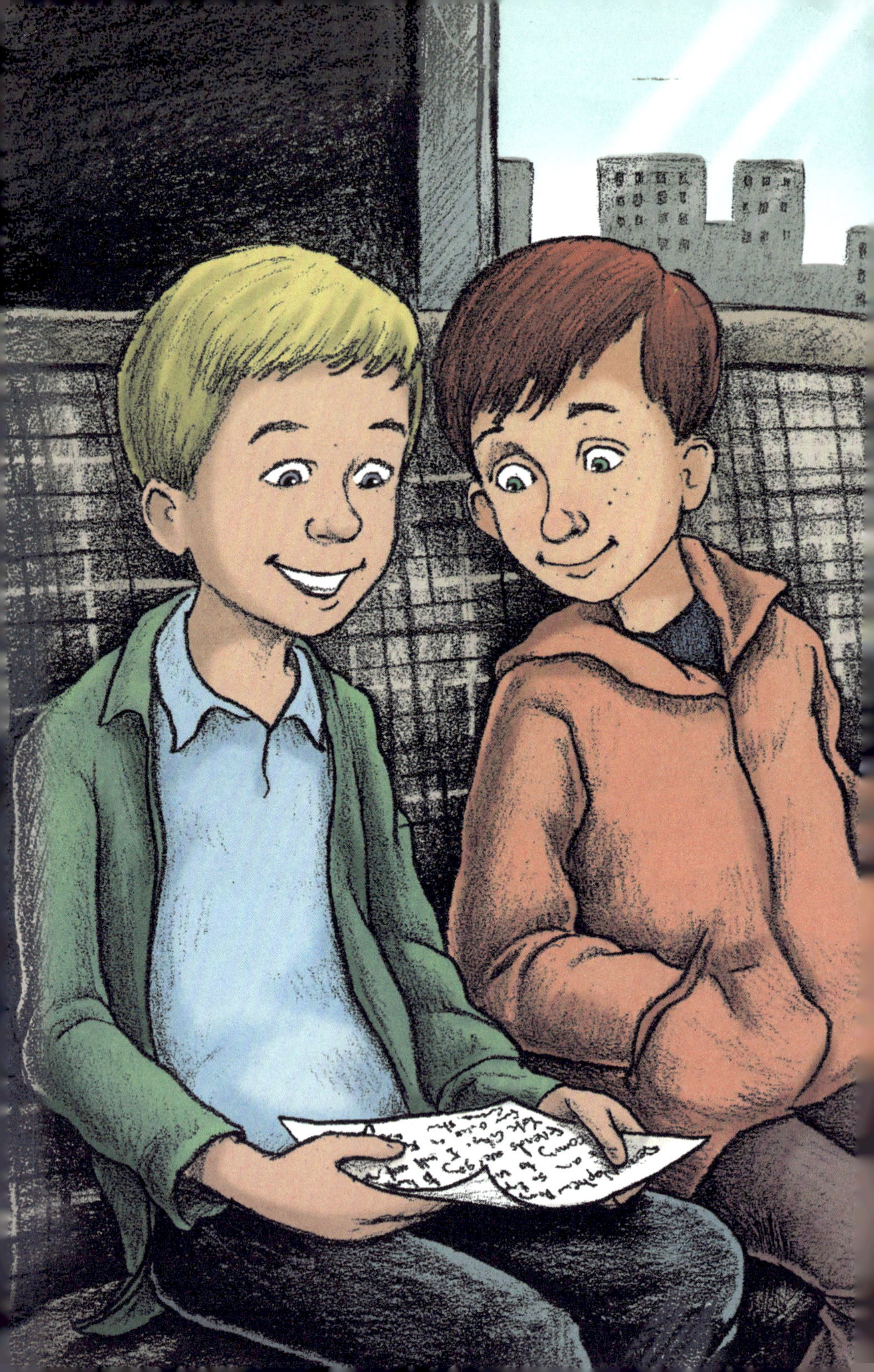

第一章

丁丁将信摊开,放在膝盖上,大声念着。

亲爱的侄子多尼:

你要来我家拜访,我很开心!你和你的朋友会喜欢纽约这座城市的。周五下午四点,我会在纽约中央车站接你们。

爱你的沃伦伯伯

乔希窃笑:"他叫你多尼吗?"

"嗯。"丁丁红着脸答,"你要是敢这么叫,我就告诉学校里的所有同学,你的中间名是卡罗尔。"

"可我的中间名不是卡罗尔!"乔希说。

丁丁脸上闪过一丝坏笑:"那又怎样?"

"伙伴们,到了!"露丝说。

火车开始减速。突然,明亮晴朗的天空消失了。火车玻璃窗外一片漆黑。

"嘿,怎么回事?"乔希惊讶地大声说。

丁丁笑了。"我们在隧道里面,乔希。"他说,"别担心。露丝和我会保护你的。"

火车速度更慢了,然后停下。"纽约中央车站!"列车员叫喊着,"终点站到了!请所有乘客下车!"

三个孩子拿起背包,跟随其他乘客来到门口。

"小心脚下。"列车员说着,帮助孩子们跳到站台上。

他们正站在一条混凝土隧道里面,火车底部散出来的灰尘和烟雾呛得丁丁直打喷嚏。

"我们去哪儿?"乔希问。

"我伯伯说他会来接咱们,"丁丁答,"或许咱们应该在这儿等着。"

他们周围的人沿着站台快步前进。丁丁踮起脚尖四处张望,但没有看见他的伯伯。

"那是你伯伯吗?"露丝问。

她指着一个穿灰色套装的矮个子男人。他正穿过人群,朝他们走来。

丁丁上蹿下跳,挥舞着手臂大喊:"沃伦伯伯,我们在这儿!"

沃伦·邓肯伯伯一头白发,满脸笑容。他手持一把雨伞,西服翻领上别着一朵红色康乃馨。

隧道的灯光照得他的眼镜闪闪发亮。

"多尼,欢迎!"他笑着对孩子们说,"坐火车怎么样?饿不饿?"

"我们很好。"丁丁答,"火车很大,妈妈还帮我打包了三明治,让我们在车上吃。"

"太好了!"丁丁的伯伯给了他一个大大的拥抱。

"这两位是谁呢?"他透过圆圆的眼镜看着他们。

"乔希和露丝,"丁丁答,"我最好的朋友!"

"真好!"沃伦伯伯说着,跟他俩握手,"现在我们去坐出租车。跟我走!"

沃伦伯伯沿着一个长长的坡向上走,孩子们跟在后面。不一会儿,他们来到一个大房间,这是丁丁第一次看见这么大的房间。

数百人行色匆匆,奔向不同方向。喇叭里传出低沉的声音,播报火车进站出站的信息。一堆堆的行李堆在光亮剔透的大理石地板上。

丁丁一个劲地看,还是目不暇接。沃伦伯伯说:"这是纽约中央车站的主楼。看上面!"

孩子们仰头朝上看……又朝上看！只见翡翠绿的天花板上舞动着金色的星星和动物。

"令人赞叹啊！"乔希说，"看，那儿有一头公牛和一只山羊！"

"是金牛座和摩羯座——十二星座中的两个，孩子。"沃伦伯伯解释，"好了，走吧！"

沃伦伯伯带着他们朝出租车走去。孩子们跟着他出去。

来到中央车站外面的大街，丁丁大为惊讶。他的耳朵里充斥着车辆的喇叭声、尖厉的刹车声、震耳的音乐声，还有食品小贩的叫卖声。

"欢迎来到'大苹果[1]'！"沃伦伯伯说。

他挥舞着手里的雨伞，吹了一声口哨。一辆黄色出租车急速驶来，吱的一声停在离沃伦伯伯锃亮的黑皮鞋几英寸[2]远的地方。

沃伦伯伯一把拉开车后门。"上车，孩子们，进去吧！"他说。

---

1. 大苹果：原文是 Big Apple，纽约的别称。——编者
2. 英寸：英美制长度单位。1 英寸 =0.0254 米。——编者

A to Z 神秘案件

他们刚坐好,关上门,出租车就左拐右拐,汇入车流中。

"去哪儿?"司机侧头问。

"西110号街,340号。"沃伦伯伯答。

他转身面对孩子们。"我们先去博物馆,"他说,"我有一件从南美洲运来的东西到了。"

司机在宽阔的大道上左拐右拐。丁丁坐直身子,鼻子贴在窗玻璃上。他看见数不清的小轿车、出租车、公交车、自行车,行人摩肩接踵。即便隔着封闭的车窗,他也感受得到这座大城市

美洲豹宝石

跳动的脉搏。

二十分钟后,出租车在一栋白色大理石建筑前猛地停下。"到了。"司机说。

沃伦伯伯递给她几张钞票:"不用找零。"

"谢谢,先生!"司机对着后视镜笑着说。

沃伦伯伯和孩子们下了车。

"这是我工作的地方。"沃伦伯伯说着,指了指绿色门旁边的一块黄铜小招牌,上面写着"波特博物馆"。

丁丁发现这里很安静。楼房前面有一排树，几个小孩正在人行道上用粉笔画画。街对面的一扇窗户里传出钢琴的演奏声。

突然，他听见响亮的招呼声："沃伦！你好！"

丁丁看见满脸笑容的一男一女站在博物馆旁边的一家小餐厅前面。

他们身后的大玻璃上方有一块招牌，上面写着"小酒馆"。

"去认识一下我的朋友。"沃伦伯伯说着,朝那对夫妻走去。

他先介绍了孩子们,然后说:"这是让－保罗和他妻子伊冯娜。"

沃伦伯伯指着招牌说:"这对可爱的夫妻经营着纽约最好的法式餐厅!"

"你们好。"夫妻俩说。

"很高兴认识你们。"孩子们异口同声地说。

伊冯娜转身面向沃伦伯伯。"你的东西送过来了!"她说,"一个又大又重的箱子。四个人一起抬到你楼上的办公室的。"

让－保罗把手伸进口袋。"我带他们进去的。他们离开后,我锁好了门。"他说着,把铜环吊着的钥匙放进沃伦伯伯手里。

"箱子里是什么?"丁丁问。

沃伦伯伯眨眨眼睛。"没什么,"他答道,"只是一些珍贵的黄金物件!"

第二章

孩子们跟随沃伦伯伯穿过绿色的门,登上铺着地毯的楼梯,来到一扇镶着磨砂玻璃窗的门前。沃伦伯伯打开门,大家走进一间宽敞但光线昏暗的办公室。

地板上放着一个有丁丁那么高的板条箱。

丁丁环顾房间。铺着东方地毯的位置上摆放了一张桌子和几把椅子。桌子旁边有一个鱼缸,里面安静地冒着泡泡。一个书柜紧靠在墙边。

透过办公室的另一扇门,丁丁看见了一台放在桌子上的电脑、一个文件柜以及一些书架。

"那是我的助理办公的地方。"沃伦伯伯说,"他下午请假了。今天是他女儿的生日,他们去了动物园。"

"你们这儿有动物园?"乔希问。

"对,曼哈顿就有一个中央公园动物园,"沃伦伯伯说,"这个动物园很小。不过纽约还有一个非常大的布朗克斯动物园!"

沃伦伯伯打开墙上的三个开关。突然,吊扇开始转动,看不见的扬声器里传出音乐,头顶的灯照射到他们身上。

"这间办公室真酷!"丁丁说。

"谢谢夸奖。"伯伯说着,指向鱼缸,"谁想喂我的小鱼?"

"我想!"露丝答道。

沃伦伯伯递给她一个装鱼饲料的容器,并给她示范撒多少到水中。

"看这个!"乔希一边说,一边拿起桌上一把闪亮的银匕首。这把匕首刀刃弯曲,把手形似一只腾飞的鹰。

"小心!"沃伦伯伯说,"这把匕首很锋利!我用它来开信封。"

"这把匕首是纯银的吗?"乔希问。

沃伦伯伯点头:"它是三百多年前西班牙制造的。"

"它能照出我的影子!"乔希说。

沃伦伯伯哈哈大笑:"那是因为我的助理每天早上都会擦拭它。"

乔希用T恤衫擦拭了一下开信刀,将它放回桌子上。

"好了,我们来看看这箱子里的东西。"沃伦伯伯说。他把西服外套搭在椅子上,然后从橱柜里拽出一个工具箱,从中拿出一把小撬棍。他把撬棍锋利的一端插进木箱的盖子下面,撬开了盖子。

箱子里面是一堆"泡沫花生[1]"。沃伦伯伯翻动着,拿出一个用牛皮纸包裹着的小物件。

1.泡沫花生:大约是带壳花生的大小和形状,一种常见的填充包装盒的缓冲材料。——编者

他撕开牛皮纸,露出里面的塑料气泡膜,然后小心翼翼地撕掉气泡膜,举起一个金杯。

"真酷!"乔希说。

沃伦伯伯对着孩子们笑。"这杯子很漂亮,对吧?"他说,"这是一个用来喝水的杯子,是在十六世纪由印加人制作的!想象一下,那几乎是五百年前的事了!你们在学校学过有关印加人的知识吗?"

孩子们摇头。

"嗯,印加人住在南美的秘鲁一带。波特博物馆即将展览一些由印加人制作的陶器和黄金雕塑。"

沃伦伯伯趴在板条箱旁边,向泡沫花生深处摸。"哈哈,这个应该是美洲豹!"

他吭哧吭哧地抱起一个更大的包装盒。那包装盒有丁丁的手臂那么长,几乎有他的腰围那么粗。沃伦伯伯把这个大包装盒砰的一声放在桌上。

"怎么这么重啊?"乔希问。

"黄金是一种很重的金属。"沃伦伯伯解释,

"印加人崇拜美洲豹的身强力壮和狡猾灵巧。这一个是纯黄金打造的,它的前爪上镶嵌了一颗极好的祖母绿宝石。"

"我们可以看看吗?"露丝问。

"可以,但要等到明天。"他说,"皮茨博士九点会到这儿来。他在印加珍宝协会工作。每件宝物出箱时都要经过皮茨博士的检查。"

"为什么？"乔希问。

"为了确保每一件宝物都被安然无恙地送达。"沃伦伯伯说，"这些都是价值连城的宝物！"

沃伦伯伯把美洲豹放回板条箱。"好好待着！"他说。

随即他把手伸进工具箱，拿出一把锤子递给乔希。"我们把杯子重新包好，放回去，然后钉紧箱子，明天再打开。"

做完这些，沃伦伯伯说："现在，让我们锁上门，步行去我的公寓。你们的背包一会儿放在罗杰那里，我要带你们去吃一顿纽约大餐！"

"罗杰是谁？"露丝问。

"他是我公寓楼的门卫。"沃伦伯伯说，"他帮房客们开门、叫出租车。"

"我们可以在你朋友开的餐厅吃晚饭吗？"乔希问。

"可以，但今晚不行。"沃伦伯伯答，"你们离开纽约前的那个晚上我再带你们去那儿吃。今晚想吃什么？"

"比萨和冰激凌！"乔希说。

丁丁哈哈大笑。"乔希什么都吃。"他说。

"我是想问，你们想吃日本菜、中国菜、意大利菜、希腊菜、印度菜，还是墨西哥菜？"沃伦伯伯问。

"为什么你不选一个呢？"丁丁说，"我们喜欢惊喜！"

沃伦伯伯关掉墙上的开关。灯、音乐和吊扇

都关上了。孩子们随他走出了办公室。

"那就给你们一个惊喜!"他一边说,一边关门。

第三章

丁丁的伯伯住在一栋低矮的灰色楼房里,离博物馆几个街区远。

一身绿色制服的高个子男子打开门。

"晚上好,邓肯先生。"男子说。

"罗杰,你好。孩子们,这是罗杰·霍巴特。"沃伦伯伯把手搭在丁丁肩上,说,"这是我侄子多尼,这两位是他的朋友乔希和露丝,他们从康涅狄格州来。"

罗杰笑看着孩子们。"欢迎来到纽约。"他说。

"我们要出去,能帮忙照看一下他们的背包吗?"沃伦伯伯说,"我要带孩子们去吃晚餐。有什么建议吗?"

罗杰摸着肚子说,"去'熊猫餐厅'吃中国菜怎么样?"

"好主意!"沃伦伯伯说,"孩子们觉得怎么样?"

"我还没吃过中国菜,"乔希说,"味道怎么样?"

"好吃,而且菜单上应有尽有。"罗杰说。

"可以!"乔希说。

"我同意。"丁丁说。

"我也同意!"露丝说,"我们是用筷子吃吗?"

沃伦伯伯笑了:"当然啦!"

他们来到一条叫"百老汇"的大街。宽敞的人行道上挤满了人。商店橱窗里闪着灯光。一个男子倚靠在一栋楼前,用萨克斯管轻柔地演奏着。装萨克斯管的盒子就敞开放在他脚边。

"看!"乔希轻声说,"这个人的盒子里有钱!"

"喜欢他演奏的人会给他一些钱。"沃伦伯伯解释道。他把一美元放进盒子里，孩子们也各自放了一些零钱，萨克斯管演奏者对他们报以微笑。

"到了。"几分钟后，沃伦伯伯说。熊猫餐

美洲豹宝石

厅有一扇闪亮的红色大门,门两边各有一只假熊猫。店主微笑着欢迎他们的到来。

两小时后,乔希仰身靠在椅子上。"我吃饱了!"他说。

服务员拿来账单,并在每人面前放了一包幸运饼干。

"饼干里夹有一张签语。"沃伦伯伯说,"有些人认为吃了饼干,签语就会成真!"

"我可以留着晚点再吃吗?"丁丁问,"我的肚子都快撑爆了!"

"好主意。我们把饼干留着,回家再吃。"沃伦伯伯说。他结账后,一行人离开了熊猫餐厅。

"顺便问一下,鸡肉上面那些黏糊糊的黑色东西是什么?"走在百老汇大街上时,乔希问。

"海藻。"丁丁说。

"不可能!"

"多尼说得对。"沃伦伯伯说,"吃海藻对身体好!"

"可能鱼吃了海藻才有好处。"乔希说。

开始下雨了,他们加快了脚步。到了公寓,罗杰把背包递给他们。"晚餐吃得怎么样?"他问。

"我吃了黑海藻。"乔希嘀咕。

罗杰咧嘴笑了。"那可是好东西,对吧?"他问。

沃伦伯伯和孩子们乘电梯来到十楼,随后沿着过道走到一扇灰色的门前。

"欢迎来到我的小公寓。"沃伦伯伯说完,带他们进去了。

沃伦伯伯的客厅里放满了各种看起来很舒适的老家具。地毯又厚实又柔软。几个书柜里摆满了书。书柜之间的白色墙壁上挂着几幅画作。

"沃伦伯伯,你家真整洁。"丁丁说。

"谢谢夸奖,多尼。露丝,你睡客房。"沃伦伯伯说,"你们两个男孩睡客厅的折叠沙发。"

大家都换好睡衣后,一起坐到餐桌旁,打开各自的幸运饼干。

"最年长的先读他的签语。"沃伦伯伯说着,掰开饼干。

他默默地读着,然后哈哈大笑。"我的签语

已经成真了。上面说我今天会遇见一些友善的人,这不是见到了你们嘛!"

"下一个是我!"乔希说。他掰开饼干,抽出那张薄薄的字条,大声朗读:"各种稀奇古怪的菜会让你开心。"

乔希做了个鬼脸。"我已经吃了海藻,"他说,"好期待接下来还会吃到什么!"

"轮到我了。"露丝说。她咬了一口饼干,看了一眼里面的字条:"啊,伙伴们。这上面说我将在意想不到的地方找到宝物!"

"侄子,该你了。"丁丁的伯伯说,"等会儿我们就要睡觉了。明天有很多事要做。"

丁丁掰开饼干,在心里默念了一遍。"我没看明白。"他说。

"大声读出来,丁丁!"乔希说。

丁丁说:"你的眼睛会欺骗你。"

伯伯笑了:"侄子,你已经睡眼惺忪了。去睡觉吧!"

第二天吃完早餐,沃伦伯伯和孩子们步行到博物馆。雨还在下,他们躲在两把伞下。

他们把滴水的雨伞放在楼梯顶部的小平台上。雨伞架上已经放了一把湿漉漉的伞。沃伦伯伯打开门,他们进入了办公室。

里面的一个人跟他们打招呼。

"啊,詹姆斯,你已经来了。"丁丁的伯伯说,"孩子们,这是我的助理詹姆斯·普赖德。詹姆斯,这是我侄子多尼·邓肯,这两位是他的朋友乔希和露丝。"

詹姆斯·普赖德微笑地看着孩子们说:"沃伦带你们到处游玩了吗?"

"还没呢。"沃伦伯伯说,"但我答应了他们,等雨停了,带他们乘轻便马车游览中央公园。"

詹姆斯敲了敲板条箱。"沃伦,这个留给你处理,"他说,"我女儿昨天在动物园玩得很开心,这让我现在有很多文件要处理。"他走进自己的办公室,关上门。

这时,办公室外面响起敲门声。沃伦伯伯打开门,一位穿着湿雨衣的男子站在门口。

"我是杰里米·皮茨博士。"男子说,"我想邓肯先生一定在等我。"

"我的确在等你,皮茨博士!"丁丁的伯伯说完,与男子握手,"快进来把身上擦干。想喝点茶吗?"

"不用,谢谢,我在宾馆吃了早餐。"皮茨博士说。他打量着办公室,然后朝大板条箱走去:"我看见这批宝物已经到了。"

"是的,箱子是昨天送过来的。"丁丁的伯伯说,"挂起你的湿衣服,我们就可以开始工作了。"

沃伦伯伯再次撬开板条箱的盖子。他从箱子里搬出一件件宝物,交给皮茨博士,博士则小心翼翼地撕开包装。他用一个特殊的放大镜,仔细

A to Z 神秘案件

检查每一件宝物，再将它们从清单上划掉。

孩子们帮忙把宝物重新包装好，包括几个黄金杯子、一些动物雕像、一些瓷器，以及一些用翡翠和羽毛做的面具。

"这些看起来都没有破损。"皮茨博士说。他瞥了一眼清单说："美洲豹在哪儿，邓肯先生？"

丁丁的伯伯把手伸向箱子深处。"多尼，你

美洲豹宝石

能帮一下我吗?"他问。

丁丁急忙过去,和伯伯一起把那个又长又重的包裹抬出板条箱。

"请放在这里。"皮茨博士说,他站在沃伦伯伯办公桌的右边。

"小心别碰着鱼缸,多尼。"把重重的包裹放在桌上时,丁丁的伯伯说。

皮茨博士撕开牛皮纸时，大伙都围过来。塑料气泡膜被揭开时，乔希长出了一口气。

这只美洲豹是纯金的，它卧坐着，红宝石做的眼睛注视前方，两只前爪之间有一颗高尔夫球那么大的祖母绿。在办公室灯光的照射下，祖母绿闪闪发亮。

"是不是令人叹为观止，孩子们？"沃伦伯伯说，"多么棒的手工艺啊！"

皮茨博士用手帕擦了擦双手，轻轻抚摸这只黄金"猫"，感受它的每一条曲线和每一处肌肉。

"这是什么？"他突然弯下腰说，看着珠宝。

"有什么不对劲吗？"丁丁的伯伯问。

皮茨博士透过放大镜观察珠宝。

一会儿，他抬起了头，看着丁丁的伯伯说："先生，这颗宝石是假的！"

第四章

"你什么意思?"丁丁的伯伯问,"我不明白这怎么会是假的。"

皮茨博士将一根手指搁在宝石上。"这不是原来那颗祖母绿。"他解释,"其实,这压根就不是祖母绿。"

"怎么可能呢?"丁丁的伯伯惊呼。

"看,我指给你看。"皮茨博士说着,从口袋里拿出一个小手电筒。

"可以帮忙拉上窗帘并关上灯吗?"他问。

丁丁离窗户最近,于是他拉上窗帘,关掉鱼缸上方的灯。乔希则赶忙关掉墙上的开关。

房间变黑了,皮茨博士打开手电筒照向宝石。

突然,手电筒的光灭了。丁丁听见有什么东西砸到了桌面,滚了下来,掉在地毯上,发出轻微的声音。

"对不起。"皮茨博士小声说,"我可能没拿稳手电筒,谁能帮我……"

"我来捡!"黑暗中乔希的声音响起。他跪在地上,在桌子底下四处摸。"找到了。"一会儿后,他说。他站起来,打开手电筒,照向桌子。

"谢谢你,小伙子。"皮茨博士说。他拿着手电筒,再次照向宝石。

"你们看,如果这是真的祖母绿,光就会透过去。"他解释,"光能透进宝石的中心。"

他用一根手指轻轻敲着宝石,说:"但这是玻璃的。注意看,灯光从表面反射回来,没有穿透宝石。"

他用手电筒照着自己的脸。

"当然，这只是我的一家之言。邓肯先生，你还可以找其他人看看。"

"那是必须的！"丁丁的伯伯说。

他走到墙边，打开灯。

房间突然变亮，丁丁眨巴了一下眼睛。他伯伯看起来很难过。

"我只是不明白真的祖母绿怎么会变成假的祖母绿！"丁丁的伯伯接着说，"你十分确定吗？"

皮茨博士点头："不好意思，我十分确定。"

"那么肯定是箱子在送来之前就被调包了。"沃伦伯伯说，"也许是在南美洲打包时被调包了。"

皮茨博士摇头："抱歉，打包时我在场。我可以肯定美洲豹被放进这个箱子时，祖母绿是真品。"

丁丁的伯伯盯着美洲豹。"我只是不明白，这怎么可能！"他重复道。

皮茨博士耸肩。"我肯定会报警。"他说，"若你还想听听其他人的意见……"

丁丁的伯伯快步走过房间，打开詹姆斯·普赖德的办公室的门。"詹姆斯，打电话给百老汇大街上的帝国珠宝,请雷吉娜·吴赶紧过来。告诉她有急事!"

等待时,皮茨博士仔细检查了办公室的门锁,然后在一个小便笺簿上记录了什么。

沃伦伯伯瘫坐在椅子上,盯着美洲豹雕像。

孩子们坐在地毯上等着。丁丁想跟伯伯说点什么,但伯伯看起来非常苦恼。

过了好久,门口传来了敲门声。沃伦伯伯一跃而起。他请进来一位身穿黑色雨衣的高个子女士。"沃伦,我争分夺秒赶过来的,"她说,"街上太拥挤了!"

两人握手,丁丁的伯伯解释了有关美洲豹宝石的情况:"皮茨博士说宝石是假的!"

"我可以看看吗?"吴女士用宝石商专用的放大镜仔细地检查了宝石好几分钟。

然后她从口袋里掏出一个小瓶子,挤出一滴液体滴在宝石上。液体挥发后,她用布擦拭了一下。

她摇着头说:"他说得对,这是玻璃仿制品。"

沃伦伯伯瘫坐在椅子上。"我都不知道该

说什么了!在哪儿调包的?如何调包的?谁会……"

"请见谅。"皮茨博士说,"门锁没有被破坏的痕迹。除了你,谁还有办公室的钥匙?"

"我的助理詹姆斯·普赖德有一把。"丁丁的伯伯说,"还有我朋友让-保罗。他挨着博物馆开了一家餐厅。昨天是他开门让搬运工进来的。"

"所以让-保罗有钥匙?"皮茨博士问。

沃伦伯伯摇头,说:"他没有钥匙。只是这批货物快到了,所以詹姆斯和我都不在博物馆时,我会把钥匙放在他那里。"

"那么除了你,还有两人可以接触到美洲豹,对吧?"皮茨博士问,"你助理和你朋友?"

"对。但我可以肯定地告诉你,他俩都不会碰这个美洲豹。这个想法太荒谬了!"

"嗯,沃伦伯伯,我能插一句话吗?"丁丁说。

大家都转身看着丁丁。

"没有指纹吗?我的意思是,如果有人拿走了真品,应该会在赝品上留下指纹,不是吗?"

一时间,众人沉默不语,然后皮茨博士对丁

丁笑了笑。"你说得很对。"他说,"我认为应该请警察来提取指纹。毫无疑问,他们会提取到我的指纹。若我猜得没错,不会有其他人的指纹。"

"你为什么这么说?"露丝问。

"小姑娘,是这样的,"皮茨博士说,"这个贼非常聪明。聪明的贼都会戴手套。"

沃伦伯伯看向电话机,点点头。"报警吧,"他对皮茨博士说,"警察会证明让－保罗和詹姆斯是无辜的!"

皮茨博士看向丁丁的伯伯:"抱歉,先生,还有一个嫌疑人。"

"是谁?"沃伦伯伯问。

"是你。"皮茨博士平静地说。

第五章

丁丁听见楼梯处传来重重的脚步声，两名警察随即进入了办公室。听完事情的经过后，警察"邀请"丁丁的伯伯去警局回答更多的问题。

"邓肯先生，你可以叫普赖德先生和让－保罗跟我们走一趟吗？"一名警察问。

"好，"丁丁的伯伯回答，"但相信我，这绝对是个可怕的误会！"

警察点头，指着雕像说："我们要把这个也带走，回警察局查验指纹。"

"那我俩呢？"雷吉娜·吴问，"皮茨博士和我可以自由离开吗？"

"我有你们的住址，"警察说，"知道去哪儿找你们。"

"那是肯定的。"皮茨博士说完，和雷吉娜·吴走了。

沃伦伯伯走到丁丁身边。"别担心，侄子，我不会去很久的。"他说，"你们和伊冯娜一起待着，等我回来。"

他弯腰拥抱丁丁时，对丁丁耳语道："多尼，别忘了你的饼干！"

詹姆斯·普赖德锁上办公室的门，一行人都下了楼。两名警察抬着重新打包好的美洲豹。

让－保罗拥抱了伊冯娜，和沃伦伯伯及詹姆斯·普赖德一起上了警察巡逻车。

雨还在下，丁丁、乔希、露丝和伊冯娜看着他们乘车而去。

"进屋吧。"伊冯娜说，"我来做点热饮喝。他们马上就会回来的。"

美洲豹宝石

她给孩子们每人一大杯热可可。四人坐在窗边，看着雨哗哗地下。

"别担心。"伊冯娜说，"等他们回来，谜团就解开了，不是吗？"

她离开孩子们，掀开一块蓝色的帘子，进了餐厅厨房。

"这太古怪了！"乔希说。

"真糟糕，"丁丁说，"我了解我的伯伯，他才不会偷什么宝石呢！"

"到底怎么回事？"露丝说，"总之有人偷走了真宝石！"

孩子们喝着热可可，透过流淌着雨水的玻璃往外看。

丁丁起身说："卫生间在哪儿？"

"问伊冯娜，"露丝说，"她可能在厨房。"

乔希喝光了杯子里的热可可。"问问她还有没有热可可！"他说。

丁丁朝餐厅后边走去，掀开蓝色帘子来到厨房。

厨房操作台上有一碗剥了皮的生洋葱，旁边

45

有一堆切好的西蓝花。他环顾四周，没看见伊冯娜。

他看见了另一块蓝色的帘子，便掀开一点朝里看，想找卫生间。

这时，他听见一阵响声。丁丁回头，看见伊冯娜从一道窄门里挤出来。那道门在她身后一关上，就看不见了。

丁丁眨了眨眼睛。门不见了！没有门框、把手和铰链。他摇头。他刚才看见什么了吗？

丁丁找到卫生间，上完厕所，赶紧回到乔希和露丝身边。

"你们听我说！"丁丁把伊冯娜和消失的门的事告诉他俩，"她关上门，门就不见了，真的！"

"消失的门？"乔希嘲笑道。

"也许那是她的私人卫生间什么的。"露丝说。

突然，丁丁想起了伯伯对他说过的话。"伯伯在楼上拥抱我时，在我耳边低语：'别忘了你的饼干。'"

乔希咧嘴一笑。"也许是他饿了呢。"他说。

"也许他是让你记住饼干里的签语！"露丝说。

美洲豹宝石

"我还留着呢!"丁丁说着,把手伸进夹克口袋。

"这是什么?"丁丁掏出了他伯伯的铜钥匙圈,"这钥匙是哪儿来的?"

"看起来像你伯伯办公室的钥匙。"乔希说。

"对!"丁丁说,"一定是他拥抱我时,放进我口袋的!"

丁丁再次把手伸进口袋里，拿出幸运饼干里的那张字条。

"你的眼睛会欺骗你。"他念道。

"你的签语成真了！"露丝说，"不知道我的能否实现。上面说我能找到一个宝物。"

"看！"乔希突然指着窗户外面说，"那位珠宝商女士！"

雷吉娜·吴急匆匆地走过餐厅。孩子们看见她溜进通往沃伦伯伯办公室的绿色的门。

"她为什么又回去了？"丁丁问。

这时，伊冯娜从蓝色帘子后面出来了。她拿着一个水壶和一盘饼干。

"再喝点热可可吗？"她问，"这儿还有我特意做的蔓越莓饼干！"

乔希和露丝伸手拿饼干时，丁丁盯着窗户外的那扇绿色的门。

突然，门开了，雷吉娜·吴出来了。她关上门，匆忙离开了这栋楼。

丁丁看见她撑着伞，步履匆匆地在街上走着。

他盯着雷吉娜·吴看。"怎么回事？"他思

考着,"明知我伯伯不在办公室,她为什么还去那儿?"

突然,一个想法冒出来了:"她就是故意趁伯伯不在的时候去办公室的。"

第六章

待伊冯娜去了厨房,丁丁把刚才看见的告诉伙伴们。

"但是办公室锁上了。"乔希说。

"也许她有钥匙呢。"丁丁说。

"她从哪儿弄来的钥匙?"乔希问,"你拿了一把,詹姆斯·普赖德拿了另一把。"

"问题是,"露丝说,"办公室空无一人,她为什么要在这个时候去那儿?"

丁丁起身。"我们得去找出答案,"他说,"或许她留下了什么线索!伊冯娜还没出来,我们现在就去。"

孩子们冲进雨中,跑到隔壁,从绿色门进入。

"看!"丁丁指着地毯说,"湿脚印!"

他们快速上楼,在楼梯顶部看见了更多湿脚印。

丁丁的手抖得厉害,他哆嗦着开了门。除了鱼缸上的一点灯光,办公室里一片漆黑。他们唯一能听见的声音来自鱼缸里冒泡的过滤器。

"这里好诡异啊。"乔希低声说。

丁丁检查地板。"这里没有湿脚印。"他轻声说。

"也许雷吉娜·吴进办公室之前擦干了鞋子。"露丝轻声回应。

"有可能。"乔希说,"但我们为什么要低声说话呢?"他打开墙上的开关,灯亮了,吊扇转动,音乐响起。

眼前突然一亮,丁丁眯了一下眼睛。"好吧,"他说,"我们四处看看。"

"看什么?"乔希问。

"我也不知道,"丁丁答,"但雷吉娜·吴来这里一定有原因。她要么拿走了什么,要么留下了什么。"

"我去检查板条箱里的东西。"露丝说,"丁丁,你为什么不检查一下詹姆斯的办公室呢?乔希,你检查垃圾桶。"

"为什么我就得去翻垃圾?"乔希问。

"因为你是一个优秀的侦探,优秀的侦探总是翻垃圾。"露丝答。

"真酷!"乔希说着,走向桌子旁的垃圾桶。

丁丁走进普赖德先生的办公室。办公室里有一张抽屉上了锁的小桌子。相框立在桌上,相片上有三个人。丁丁认出其中一人是詹姆斯·普赖德。他猜测那位女士和那个孩子是普赖德的妻子和女儿。

丁丁先检查了角落里的一个灰色文件柜,柜子上了锁。接着,他用手指摸索书架,翻开了一些书,查看里面是否夹着东西——虽然他也不知道要找什么。他甚至掀开地毯看了看。他不知道是否有东西被偷，也没找到任何线索。

正要离开时，丁丁注意到有一面墙看起来与其他墙不太一样。他盯着看了一会儿，试图弄明白哪里不对劲。

随即他想到了：这面墙前没有摆放书架和文件柜，墙上也没有挂画作，什么都没有！它就是一面光秃秃的墙。

丁丁走近，用手指摸着条纹壁纸。在高于头顶的地方，他摸到了一条细小的缝。沿着细缝继续摸，他又摸到了另一条缝，这条缝一直延伸到地面。反方向两英尺[1]的地方，还有第三条缝延伸到地面。这些缝几乎都藏在墙纸里面。

丁丁往后一跳，就像手被烧着了似的。"伙伴们！"他大声喊。

乔希和露丝跑进詹姆斯的办公室。

丁丁指引他们看缝隙。"我觉得这是一扇暗门！"他说。

他试着把手指塞进缝隙，但是门一动不动。

---

1. 英尺：英美制长度单位。1 英尺 =0.3048 米。——编者

A to Z 神秘案件

"如果这面墙后面有楼梯,"露丝说,"可能正好通向伊冯娜的厨房的暗门!"

乔希睁大双眼:"那就是说,她没有钥匙也能进来!"

"你们说,我在楼下看见她的时候,她是不是刚刚从这儿出去?"丁丁问。

"也许她刚和雷吉娜·吴见了面!"露丝说,"可能是伊冯娜让雷吉娜·吴进来的。"

"有可能。"丁丁说着,回到伯伯的办公室,

美洲豹宝石

"但是为什么呢?我们还得好好找找。乔希,你在垃圾桶里发现了什么吗?"

"一无所获。"乔希答。

露丝刚才坐的位置上,有一堆泡沫花生。她打开了每一件物品的包装,检查后放在了旁边。

"我刚看到的都是昨天见过的那些物品,"她说,"我觉得没有丢失什么。"

孩子们继续搜寻。窗帘后面和东方地毯下面都搜过了。他们把每张桌子的抽屉里的东西都掏出来了。他们甚至还挖了挖窗户边上的花盆里的泥土。

"除了一扇打不开的暗门,我们什么也没找到。"乔希嘀咕着。

"我们又不能当着伊冯娜的面检查楼下厨房里的那扇门。"露丝说。

"现在怎么办?"乔希问。

"不知道,"丁丁说,他看着乔希和露丝,"但我伯伯指望咱们在这儿发现一些情况呢。找不到我不会罢休的!"

第七章

"但是我们全搜遍了。"乔希说着,躺倒在地毯上。

露丝走到鱼缸边,拿起鱼食袋。

"真奇怪,"她说,"水面上漂着一些鱼食。你们谁喂过鱼吗?"

"我没喂。"丁丁说。

"我也没喂。"乔希说。

露丝看着漂在水面上的鱼食说:"那么,有人来喂了。"

"也许是鱼仙子做的。"乔希说。

"啊,我的天!"露丝尖叫。

"怎么了?"丁丁问。乔希一跃而起,和丁丁快步走上前。

"看鱼缸底部!"露丝说。她指着水底。

乔希把鼻子贴在鱼缸的玻璃上。"看起来像一堆石头。"他说。

露丝皱眉。"谁去关下灯。"她说。

乔希推了一下丁丁。"去,小笨蛋!"

丁丁迅速走到墙边关掉开关。音乐、吊扇和灯都关闭了。

露丝指着鱼缸底部。"看见那颗亮闪闪的绿色石头了吗?我觉得它就是丢失的宝石!"

丁丁用胳膊肘把乔希推开,盯着石头看。"不是吧,这颗太大了。"他说,"那颗宝石像一个高尔夫球,记得吗?"

"水下的东西都显大,"露丝说,"你的双眼又骗你了,丁丁!"

露丝把手伸到鱼缸底部,取出那颗绿色石头。她用牛仔服擦干石头时,水滴到了地板上。

美洲豹宝石

从水里拿出后,这颗石头看起来与鱼缸里的其他石头不一样。在鱼缸灯光的照射下,这颗石头呈鲜艳的绿色。

"哇!"丁丁说,"真漂亮!"

"这颗宝石怎么会在鱼缸里呢?"乔希问。

"我猜是小偷扔在里面的。"丁丁答。

"但小偷怎么会这么做呢?"乔希问。

露丝摇头说:"也许他要快速找到一个地方藏起这颗宝石。"

丁丁点头说:"詹姆斯今天一大早就在这儿。也许他偷宝石的时候,我们恰好到了!"

"我去开灯。"乔希说着,朝墙上的开关走去。

"别动!"丁丁突然说,"什么声音?"

"什么声音?"乔希问着,打开吊扇、音乐和灯的开关。

丁丁走过去,又关掉了这些开关。"听,"黑暗中他轻声说,"听见了吗?"

"我好像听见了,"露丝说,"像是'嗡嗡嗡'的声音。"

"或许是鱼缸在响。"乔希说。

露丝关掉起泡器。"不是，还有嗡嗡声。"她说。

"我现在也听见了。"乔希说，"是什么在响呢？带电的都关了！"

"我去开灯。"丁丁说。

屋内亮了，三个孩子在办公室四处搜索起来。

丁丁在书架前停下："伙伴们，这边更响！"

乔希窃笑。"《嗡嗡作响的书案件》！"他说。

丁丁踮起脚尖，双手在书架顶部摸索。他摸到一个小开关，按了一下。突然，一个书架打开了。"看！"他惊讶地喊。

"嘿！那些书是假的！"乔希说，"这是一个密室。"

假书后面有一台小电视机和一台录像机。密室打开后，嗡嗡声更响了。然后录像机发出"咔嗒"一声，嗡嗡声停止了。

"这是在倒带，"乔希说，"一定是带子录完了。我爸爸的录像机也是这样的。"

"嗯，但是正在倒的是什么内容呢？"丁丁问。

接着录像机又发出"咔嗒"一声。孩子们看

见一个红灯亮起,录像机显示屏上的数字开始计数:01,02,03……

"嘿!"乔希说,"机器正在录像!"

"也许你伯伯考虑到了安全问题,特意放了一个录像机在这儿。"露丝说。

"可能如你所说,露丝。"丁丁说着,看向天花板,"办公室的某处一定安装了摄像头。"

"你觉得我们被摄像头拍到了?"露丝说,"那看一看录像吧!"

"好主意!"乔希说。

丁丁迅速把录像带倒到开头处,然后打开电视机,按动录像机上的播放键。

屏幕上出现了图像,不一会儿就播到了他们站在电视机和录像机前面的画面。

"真酷!"乔希说。

随后画面跳跃切换,切换到空无一人、漆黑一片的办公室的画面。之后他们看见办公室门开了,詹姆斯·普赖德走了进来。

"这应该是录的今天早些时候,"露丝说,"詹姆斯比我们早到。"

"也许录到了他偷宝石的经过!"乔希说。

他们看见詹姆斯走到墙边开了灯,然后他脱下雨衣,进了自己的办公室。

"按快进键,"乔希说,"咱们快速看看发生了什么。"

丁丁按动按键,录像带快速转动,屏幕上的图像也在闪动。

"看!"露丝说,"有情况!"

丁丁赶紧按下播放键。录像带慢下来了,孩

子们看见他们和沃伦伯伯走进办公室的画面。

他们盯着看，又看见他们与詹姆斯·普赖德见面的画面，接着沃伦伯伯请皮茨博士进来，板条箱再次被打开了，皮茨博士检查每一件包装好的物品。

"此时我们把美洲豹从箱子里拿出来了。"丁丁说。

"博士告诉我们那颗宝石是假的。"乔希补充。

露丝指着屏幕说："这时他拿出手电筒。"

"丁丁和我拉上窗帘，关了灯。"乔希说。

画面变黑了。

接着，他们看见皮茨博士的手电筒发出了光，紧接着光没了。

"这时你帮他找到了手电筒。"露丝对乔希说。

没一会儿，皮茨博士又拿到了手电筒，对着美洲豹宝石照。

接着办公室的灯亮了。雷吉娜·吴很快就来了，然后警察也来了。录像显示所有人都离开了办公室。

丁丁伸手去按停止键。

"等一下!"露丝说,"伊冯娜和雷吉娜·吴呢?"

"哦,是的。"丁丁说,"还好你想到了,露丝。"

他们盯着录像里的空办公室看了一会儿。丁丁正要快进时,看见詹姆斯·普赖德办公室的门开了,伊冯娜进来了!

"那扇暗门确实通往伊冯娜的厨房!"露丝说。

他们看见伊冯娜穿过办公室,径直朝鱼缸走去!到了鱼缸边,伊冯娜对着鱼儿噘嘴叫。然后她拿起鱼食,往鱼缸里撒了一些,转身离开。

孩子们相互看着。"我猜她不是小偷。"乔希说。

露丝转向电视机。"雷吉娜·吴呢?"她问。

他们又看了一会儿录像,但是雷吉娜·吴没再出现。最后,他们看见自己进了办公室。

丁丁暂停了录像带,按了倒带键。

"我在想,你伯伯为什么不告诉警察这里有录像?"乔希说,"警察如果看了录像,至少能知道詹姆斯和伊冯娜没有偷宝石。"

丁丁点头。"伊冯娜不知道宝石在鱼缸里面,"

他说,"所以我敢说不是让－保罗放进去的。"

丁丁面露忧愁:"假如雷吉娜·吴都没进办公室……"

露丝抽了一口气:"那就意味着——"

"那就意味着我伯伯是唯一的嫌疑人。"丁丁说。

第八章

乔希张大嘴巴。"你伯伯是小偷吗?"他问。

"乔希!"露丝用责备的语气喊,转身面对丁丁。"你伯伯不是小偷,"她说,"他根本没有机会拿走宝石。他开板条箱时,我们也在旁边,刚才看的录像里他确实没有拿。"

丁丁只要一想到伯伯有可能偷走了宝石,心里就不舒服。"在我们关了所有灯的时候呢?"他问。

"但就一小会儿的时间,"露丝说,"我想不明白他怎么——"

"伙伴们!办公桌!"乔希突然说,"看啊!看见有什么不同了吗?"

丁丁和露丝看着沃伦伯伯的办公桌。

"什么意思?"丁丁问,"桌上只是少了记事簿和开信刀,其他的与昨天和今天上午一模一样啊。"

乔希按下录像机上的播放键。他快进到大家都在办公室的那个画面。

"看!"过了一会儿,他大声说,"看开信刀。刀尖对着窗户,对吧?"

"对,所以呢?"丁丁说。

"等下你就明白了。"

录像中,灯被关掉了。皮茨博士用手电筒照完宝石,灯又亮了。

"现在看!"乔希激动地说,"看见了吧,开信刀的刀尖对着与窗户相反的方向。它转了个身!"

"这有什么关系吗,乔希?"露丝问。

"不知道,"乔希说,"但是有人在关灯时拿了开信刀,又放了回去。"

"当时谁离开信刀最近?"丁丁问着,依次按下暂停键和倒带键。

"我记得皮茨博士离刀最近,"乔希说,"他就站在美洲豹前面。开信刀就离他几英寸远。"

"但是一片漆黑,他拿开信刀干什么呢?"露丝问。

这时,他们听见办公室门口传来重重的脚步声,似乎有人在地毯上跺脚。

"是谁?"露丝小声问。

乔希倒吸了一口气:"门锁了吗?"

"没锁!"丁丁小声回应。他挥起一只手,关掉了墙上的开关。室内漆黑一片,只有鱼缸上的小灯亮着。

"看!"乔希低声说。透过门上的磨砂玻璃窗,孩子们看见一个高高的身影。

他们听见"咔嗒"一声,门把手被转动了。

"快躲起来!"丁丁小声说,"躲到詹姆斯的办公室里!"

美洲豹宝石

　　孩子们冲进小办公室。丁丁将门虚掩，留了一道缝，以便看看是谁进来了。
　　是皮茨博士。

第九章

  皮茨博士潜入漆黑的办公室。孩子们看见他慢慢地朝沃伦伯伯的办公桌走去。
  突然，他打开手电筒，慢慢转身，照向房间各处。
  在詹姆斯的办公室里，丁丁缩到墙边，屏住呼吸，感觉旁边的乔希和露丝也吓得发抖。
  丁丁壮着胆子再次往外瞄。手电筒被放在桌上，在鱼缸上投下一个黄色的光圈。

皮茨博士蹲下，盯着鱼缸看。

突然，他骂了一句。丁丁看见皮茨博士拿起手电筒，挥舞着照向屋内的各个地方。

丁丁僵住了，不敢呼吸。他再次往外瞄，看见皮茨博士正用手电筒照着脚边的地板。

他弯下腰，触摸地板。

丁丁想起露丝刚滴了一些水在那儿。

皮茨博士又用手电筒照向漆黑的办公室，最终照向了詹姆斯办公室的门。

"谁在里面？"皮茨博士问。

丁丁闭上眼睛。他感觉自己全身冰凉。露丝无力地叹了一口气。

接着，丁丁听见脚步声，皮茨博士正朝他们躲藏的地方走来。

"我们必须离开这里！"丁丁心想。他贴紧墙壁，但是墙壁突然不见了！

丁丁察觉到一只有力的手抓住了他的胳膊，另一只手捂住了他的嘴巴。丁丁挣扎着，感觉自己在被人往后拖。

"别说话！"嘶哑的声音在他耳边响起，"跟我走！"

丁丁太害怕了，不敢反抗，听话地跟着。他伸手去摸乔希和露丝，但没摸到。"他俩去哪儿了？"

"下楼，快点！"那个声音又说。

丁丁察觉到脚下是楼梯。他跌跌撞撞地下楼，闻到了熟悉的味道。

下到最后一级台阶，一扇门开了。丁丁看见了亮光，闻到了洋葱的味道。

他在伊冯娜的厨房！

乔希和露丝随即围了上来。伊冯娜松开丁丁的胳膊，用力关紧门。这就是丁丁曾见她关闭的那扇小门。

"走。"伊冯娜说着，将手指放在嘴边，示意大家别出声。

伊冯娜带着他们快速来到餐厅前面。

"小偷还在上面。"她说，"我必须把外面的门关上。这样小偷就被困在里面了，对吧？"

她快步朝餐厅出口走去，但此时皮茨博士已经从餐厅窗户外跑过去了。

美洲豹宝石

"他跑了!"伊冯娜哀号道,"现在我们抓不到他了!"

"没关系。"丁丁笑着说,"我觉得录像机录到了他。"

"录像机?"伊冯娜问,"我不明白。"

"我伯伯在办公室里安装了一个隐蔽的摄像头。"丁丁解释。

他看着乔希和露丝。"咱们藏起来之前,我按了倒带键,记得吗?我确定录像带倒到了最前面,皮茨博士进来后,它又开始录像了。"

"不仅如此,"乔希说,"开信刀上应该有他的指纹!"

"开信刀?"伊冯娜看着三个孩子。

"我明白是怎么回事了。"露丝说,"关灯时,他一定是用开信刀把宝石从美洲豹的爪子上撬下来了。然后他快速替换上假宝石,把真的放进了鱼缸里。"

"假如他把宝石拿走了,"伊冯娜说,"摄像头和指纹又有什么用呢?"

"他没有拿走!"露丝说着,张开手,把宝石亮给伊冯娜看。

"真宝石在鱼缸里,我先拿出来了!"

"真棒!"伊冯娜说完,拥抱了露丝。

"现在怎么办?"乔希问。

伊冯娜走向墙上的电话机。"报警!"她说。

第十章

让-保罗端起水杯。"咱们干杯!"他说。

沃伦伯伯和伊冯娜端起杯子。

"敬三个勇敢聪明的孩子!"让-保罗说着,看向丁丁、乔希和露丝。

"听我说,"沃伦伯伯说,"你们把一个小偷送进了监狱,使一颗无价的宝石免遭盗窃。"

"多亏了你让我别忘记幸运饼干。"丁丁对伯伯说。

丁丁的伯伯笑了:"我知道,把钥匙留给你,提醒你不要随便相信眼睛所看见的,你就能找出真相。"

"露丝的幸运饼干说,她会在意想不到的地方找到宝物,"乔希说,"她真的找到了!"

"乔希发现开信刀被移动了。"露丝说。

"是的,丁丁还发现了书后面的录像机。"乔希说。

丁丁笑着对伊冯娜说:"谢天谢地,多亏你救了我们!"

"当时我准备再拿些饼干给你们吃,结果你们走了,"伊冯娜说,"然后我看见那个博士鬼鬼祟祟地进了楼下的门。于是我赶紧从后面的楼梯跑了上去!"

"为什么这里有那些暗门?"露丝问丁丁的伯伯。

"多年前,波特博物馆是一栋私宅,"他解释,"老波特夫妇的仆人们都是从后面的楼梯上上下下。后来波特私宅成了博物馆,建筑师们决定保留这些门和楼梯。"

"他们的决定真明智!"乔希说。

美洲豹宝石

"我不在时,伊冯娜会上来喂鱼。"沃伦伯伯说。

伊冯娜笑了:"你之前可能以为是我拿走了宝石,对吧?"

丁丁脸红了:"是的,后来我看见雷吉娜·吴偷偷进来了,我也想过是她!"

沃伦伯伯哈哈大笑。"她刚打电话来解释了,"他说,"她的雨伞落在这里,所以回来拿伞。"

"沃伦伯伯,"丁丁说,"你为什么不告诉警察这里有摄像头和录像呢?"

沃伦伯伯笑了。"我完全忘记了这里有摄像头!"他说,"而且,我对电子产品一窍不通。那是詹姆斯安装的,但是他也忘记了。"

"有一个地方我想不明白,皮茨博士怎么能那么快地调换宝石呢?"乔希说,"室内那么黑。"

"我确定他练习过。"沃伦伯伯说,"他一进来,就看到了我桌上的开信刀。"

"所以他要我们把美洲豹放在鱼缸旁边的桌子上,"丁丁说,"他知道可以把宝石放到鱼缸里。"

伯伯点头:"是的,晚点他再来取走。"

"所以他叫你另找人来鉴定,"露丝说,"那时宝石确实是假的。因为他已经拿走了真的,对吧?"

"对!"沃伦伯伯说,"差点就让他得逞了。"

他满脸笑容,看着一起进餐的孩子们说:"但是他没想到詹姆斯的办公室里藏了三个侦探!"

这时，他们听见餐厅外面响起铃铛声。

"哈哈，我们的车来了！"沃伦伯伯起身说。

"什么车？"丁丁问，"我们不是步行回你的公寓吗？"

"现在不回去，侄子。"伯伯说，"走！"

他领着大伙来到外面。一匹白色大马正立

A to Z 神秘案件

在一旁等候，它后面拉着一辆双轮轻便马车，皮革马具上挂着小灯和小铃铛。

一个矮个子男人从驾驶位上下来。他穿着一身干净利落的灰色套装，戴着一顶黑色大礼帽。

"你们好，我是阿尔菲。"男子说，"这匹出色的马叫王子。"

"爬上去！"沃伦伯伯说。

"真酷！"乔希爬上马车说，"我们去哪儿？"

"去哪儿都行。"露丝说着，爬到乔希旁边坐下。

美洲豹宝石

沃伦伯伯帮助丁丁上去,然后坐在他身旁。

"我们去看纽约城的夜景,"他说,"我可不想你们就这么回家了,认为这里只有喧嚣的车辆

和偷宝石的贼!"

他拍了一下马车后部:"走啦,阿尔菲!"

"再见!"伊冯娜和让-保罗站在路边用法语大声说,"明天见!"

阿尔菲对着王子发出啧啧声,马车缓缓移动。马咯噔咯噔地在街上慢慢走着。

丁丁靠着座椅后背,抬头看着天空。无数的星星向他闪烁。其中一颗星星比其他的更大,看起来是绿色的,就像一颗宝石。

绿色星星闪了一下,消失了。

丁丁笑了。

"有什么好笑的?"乔希问。

丁丁摇头。"没什么,"他说,"我的眼睛又在骗我了。"

A to Z Mysteries®

The Jaguar's Jewel

by **Ron Roy**

illustrated by
John Steven Gurney

CANADA
ME
VT
NH
NY
MA
GREEN LAWN
CT
RI
NEW YORK CITY
PA
NJ
EW JERSEY
Welcome to
A to Z Mysteries
on Location
at NEW YORK CITY
N
W
E
S

PORTER MUSEUM
LE PETIT BISTRO
SUBWAY
UNCLE WARREN'S APT
CENTRAL PARK
ROOSEVELT ISLAND
PANDA PALACE
BROADWAY
AMERICAN MUSEUM OF NATURAL HISTORY
ZOO
TAXI
EMPIRE JEWELRY
UNITED NATIONS
GRAND CENTRAL STATION
TIMES SQUARE
EMPIRE STATE BLDG
WORLD TRADE CENTER
MANHATTAN BRIDGE
BROOKLYN BRIDGE

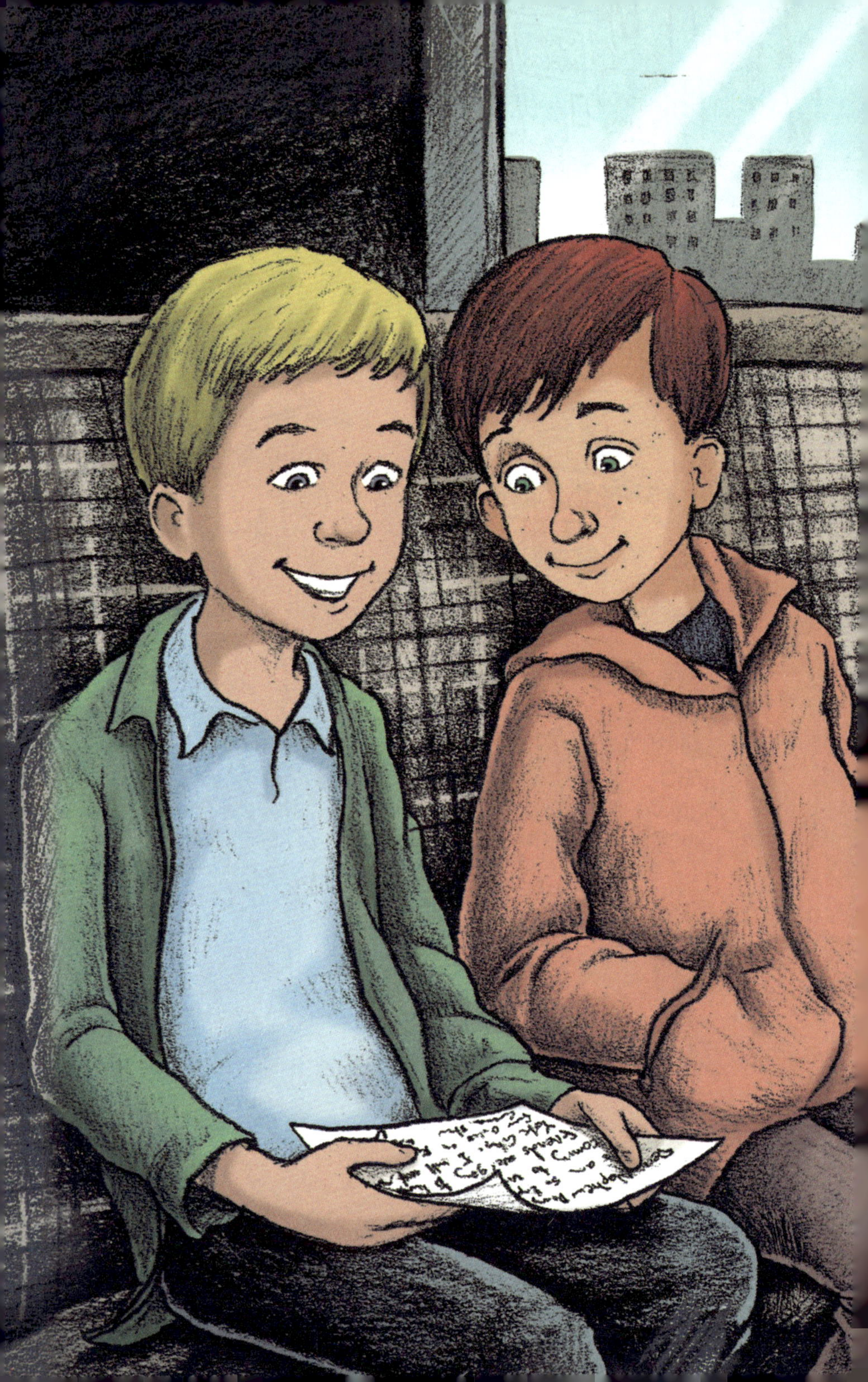

Chapter 1

Dink spread the note on his knees and read it out loud.

Dear Nephew Donny,
I am so happy that you're coming to visit! You and your friends are going to love New York City. I will meet your train at four o'clock on Friday, at Grand Central Station.

Love,
Uncle Warren

Josh giggled. "He calls you Donny?"

"Yeah," Dink said, blushing. "But if you ever do, I'll tell all the kids at school your middle name is Carol."

"But my middle name isn't Carol!" Josh said.

Dink flashed an evil grin. "So?"

"Guys, I think we're there," Ruth Rose said.

The train slowed. Suddenly, the bright, sunny day vanished. Everything outside the train windows turned black.

"Hey, what happened?" Josh cried.

Dink laughed. "We're in a tunnel, Josh," he said. "Don't worry. Ruth Rose and I will protect you."

The train slowed even more, then stopped. "New York, Grand Central Station!" the conductor called. "Last stop! All passengers off!"

The kids grabbed their backpacks and followed the other passengers to the door.

"Watch your step," the conductor said. He helped the kids hop onto the platform.

They found themselves standing in a concrete tunnel. The dust and soot coming up from under the train made Dink sneeze.

"Where do we go?" Josh asked.

"My uncle said he'd meet us," Dink said. "Maybe we should just wait here."

All around them, people were hurrying along the platform. Dink stood on tiptoe, but he couldn't see his uncle anywhere.

"Is that him?" Ruth Rose asked.

She pointed to a short man in a gray suit. He was pushing toward them through the crowd.

Dink jumped up and down and waved. "Uncle Warren, here we are!"

Uncle Warren Duncan had white hair and a big smile. He carried an umbrella and wore a red carnation in his lapel. His eyeglasses twinkled in the underground lights.

"Donny, welcome!" he said, beaming at the kids. "How was your train ride? Are you hungry?"

"We're fine," Dink said. "The train was great, and Mom packed sandwiches for us."

"Splendid!" Dink's uncle gave him a big hug.

"And whom have we here?" he asked, peering through his round glasses.

"Josh and Ruth Rose," Dink said, "my best friends!"

美洲豹宝石

"Marvelous!" Uncle Warren said, shaking their hands. "Now let's go find a cab. Follow me!"

Uncle Warren marched up a long ramp with the kids right behind him. A moment later, they entered the biggest room Dink had ever seen.

Hundreds of people bustled in every direction. A deep voice announcing train arrivals and departures echoed over a loudspeaker. Piles of luggage were heaped around the gleaming marble floor.

Try as he might, Dink couldn't take it all in. Uncle Warren said, "This is Grand Central Station's main terminal. Look up!"

The kids tipped their heads back and looked up…and up! Gold-painted stars and animals danced across an emerald green ceiling.

"This is so awesome!" Josh said. "Look, there's a bull and a goat!"

"Taurus and Capricorn—the zodiac signs, dear boy," Uncle Warren explained. "Now onward!"

Uncle Warren marched them toward an exit. The kids followed him out of the building.

The street outside Grand Central Station was a shock to Dink. His ears were blasted by horns honking, brakes squealing, music blaring, and food vendors shouting.

"Welcome to the Big Apple!" Uncle Warren said.

He waved his umbrella and whistled. A yellow cab zoomed up and screeched to a halt inches from Uncle Warren's shiny black shoes.

Uncle Warren yanked open the rear door. "In, youngsters, in!" he cried.

They had barely sat down and shut the door when the cab lurched back into traffic.

"Where to?" the driver asked over her shoulder.

"Number three forty, West One Hundred and Tenth Street," Uncle Warren said.

He turned to the kids. "We'll stop at the museum first," he said. "I'm expecting a shipment from South America."

Dink sat up as the driver zigzagged her way up a wide avenue. With his nose to the glass, Dink watched thousands of cars, taxis, buses, bikes, and people dodge one another. Even through the closed taxi window, he could feel the throbbing pulse of the huge city.

Twenty minutes later, the cab hurtled to a stop in front of a building made of white marble. "Here we are," the driver said.

Uncle Warren handed her a few bills. "Keep the change, please."

"Thanks, mister!" the driver said, smiling into her rearview mirror.

Uncle Warren and the kids piled out of the taxi.

"This is where I work," Uncle Warren said. He pointed to a small brass sign next to a green door. The sign read THE PORTER MUSEUM.

Dink noticed that it was a lot quieter here. Trees stood in front of the buildings, and a few kids were drawing chalk pictures on the sidewalk. From a window across the street came the sound of someone playing a piano.

Suddenly, he heard a voice call out, "Warren! Hello!"

94

美洲豹宝石

Dink saw a smiling man and woman standing in front of a small restaurant next to the museum.

Behind them, a sign above a wide window read LE PETIT BISTRO.

"Come meet my friends," Uncle Warren said, heading toward the couple.

He introduced the kids. "And this is Jean-Paul and his wife, Yvonne," Uncle Warren said.

Uncle Warren pointed to the sign. "These lovely people own the best French restaurant in New York!"

"Hello," the man and woman said, smiling.

"Nice to meet you," the kids said all together.

Yvonne turned to Uncle Warren. "It came!" she said. "A big, heavy box. Four men carried it upstairs to your office."

Jean-Paul reached into his pocket. "I went up with them, then locked the door when they left," he said, dropping a key on a brass ring into Uncle Warren's hand.

"What's in the box?" Dink asked.

Uncle Warren winked. "Nothing much," he said. "Only priceless gold!"

Chapter 2

The kids followed Uncle Warren through the green door. They climbed carpeted stairs to a door with a frosted-glass window. Uncle Warren unlocked it, and they walked into a spacious, dimly lit office.

A wooden crate nearly as tall as Dink sat on the floor.

Dink looked around the room. A desk and some chairs were arranged on an Oriental rug. A fish tank bubbled quietly near the desk. Against one wall stood a bookcase.

Dink peeked through another door and saw a computer on a desk, a file cabinet, and some bookshelves.

"My assistant works in there," Uncle Warren said. "He took the afternoon off. It's his daughter's birthday, and they've gone to the zoo."

"You have a zoo?" Josh asked.

"Yes, right here in Manhattan we have the Central Park Zoo," Uncle Warren said. "It's pretty small, but there's also the Bronx Zoo, which is enormous!"

Uncle Warren flipped up three switches on the wall. Suddenly, a ceiling fan began whirring around. Music came from hidden speakers. Overhead lights beamed down on them.

"This is a cool office!" Dink said.

"Thank you," his uncle said. He pointed to the fish tank. "Who'd like to feed my little friends?"

"I would!" Ruth Rose said.

Uncle Warren handed her a container of fish food and showed her how much food to sprinkle on the water.

"Look at this!" Josh said, lifting a shiny silver dagger off the desk. The blade was curved, and the handle was shaped like a soaring hawk.

"Careful," Uncle Warren said. "It's sharp! I use it as a letter opener."

"Is it real silver?" Josh asked.

Uncle Warren nodded. "It was made in Spain more than three hundred years ago."

"I can see my reflection in it!" Josh said.

Uncle Warren laughed. "That's because my assistant polishes it every morning."

Josh wiped the letter opener on his T-shirt and placed it back on the desk.

"Now, let's see what we have here," Uncle Warren said. He draped his suit jacket over a chair, then dragged a toolbox from a closet. He selected a small crowbar from among the tools. Fitting the sharp end of the bar under the crate's lid, he pried the top off.

Inside were mounds of white packing "peanuts." Uncle Warren reached through the peanuts and pulled out a small package wrapped in brown paper.

He stripped away the paper to reveal a layer of plastic bubble wrap. He carefully removed the plastic and held up a gold cup.

"Cool!" said Josh.

Uncle Warren grinned at the kids. "Lovely, isn't it?" he said. "This is a drinking cup made by the Incan people in the fifteen hundreds. Imagine, almost five hundred years ago! Have you studied the Incas in school?"

The kids shook their heads.

"Well, the Incas lived in Peru, in South America. The Porter Museum is going to display some of their pottery and gold sculpture."

Leaning over the side of the crate, Uncle Warren dug deeper into the peanuts. "Aha, I think this is the jaguar!"

Grunting, he lifted out a much bigger package. It was as long as Dink's arm and nearly as big around as his waist. The heavy package made a solid thud as Uncle Warren set it on his desk.

"Why's it so heavy?" Josh asked.

"Gold is a heavy metal," Uncle Warren explained.

"The Incas admired jaguars for their strength and cunning. This one is made of solid gold. It holds a fabulous emerald in its front paws."

"Can we see it?" asked Ruth Rose.

"Yes, but not until tomorrow," he said. "A Dr. Pitts will be here at nine o' clock. He works for the Society of Incan Treasures. Dr. Pitts will inspect every piece as it comes out of its wrapping."

"Why?" Josh asked.

"To make sure everything has arrived safely,"

Uncle Warren said. "These pieces are priceless treasures!"

Uncle Warren put the jaguar back in the crate. "Sleep well!" he said.

Then he reached into the toolbox and handed Josh a hammer. "Let's rewrap the cup and put it back, then nail the crate shut again till tomorrow."

After they'd finished, Uncle Warren said, "Now let's lock up and walk to my apartment. We'll leave your backpacks with Roger, then I'll treat you to a

New York dinner!"

"Who's Roger?" Ruth Rose asked.

"He's the doorman at my apartment building," Uncle Warren said. "He opens the door for tenants and whistles for taxis."

"Can we eat at your friends' restaurant?" Josh asked.

"Yes, but not tonight," Uncle Warren said. "I'm saving that for your last night in the city. What kind of food do you like?"

"Pizza and ice cream!" Josh said.

Dink laughed. "Josh will eat anything," he said.

"I mean, do you want Japanese, Chinese, Italian, Greek, Indian, or Mexican food?" Dink's uncle asked.

"Why don't you pick?" Dink said. "We love surprises!"

Uncle Warren flipped down the wall switches. The lights, music, and ceiling fan all went off. The kids followed him out of the office.

"Then a surprise you shall have!" he said, and pulled the door shut behind them.

Chapter 3

Dink's uncle lived in a squat gray building a few blocks from the museum.

A tall man in a green uniform opened the doors.

"Good evening, Mr. Duncan," the man said.

"Hello, Roger. Kids, this is Roger Hobart." Uncle Warren put his hand on Dink's shoulder. "This is my nephew, Donny, and these are his pals from Connecticut, Josh and Ruth Rose."

Roger smiled at the kids. "Welcome to New York,"

he said.

"Will you watch their backpacks while we're out?" Uncle Warren asked. "I'm taking the kids for dinner. Any suggestions?"

Roger rubbed his stomach. "How about the Panda Palace, for Chinese?"

"Perfect!" Uncle Warren said. "How about it, kids?"

"I've never eaten Chinese food," Josh said. "What's it like?"

"Delicious, and there are about a million choices on the menu," Roger said.

"All right!" Josh said.

"I'm game," Dink said.

"Me too!" Ruth Rose said. "Can we eat with chopsticks?"

Uncle Warren laughed. "Of course!"

They walked to a street called Broadway. The wide sidewalks were crowded with people. Lights began to come on in store windows. A man leaned against a building, playing softly on a saxophone. The saxophone case lay open at his feet.

美洲豹宝石

"Look!" Josh whispered. "There's money in that guy's case!"

"If people like his playing, they give him money," Uncle Warren explained. He dropped a dollar bill into the case. The kids each dropped some change in, getting a smile from the sax player.

"Here we are," Uncle Warren said a few minutes later. The Panda Palace had a shiny red door with fake panda bears standing on either side. A smiling host welcomed them to the restaurant.

Two hours later, Josh leaned back from the table. "I'm stuffed!" he said.

Their waitress brought the bill and placed a fortune cookie in front of each of them.

"Inside these cookies you'll find a slip of paper telling your fortune," Uncle Warren said. "Some people think that if you eat the cookie, your fortune will come true!"

"Can I save mine till later?" Dink asked. "My stomach is ready to bust!"

"Good idea. We'll have the cookies at home," Uncle Warren said. He paid the bill, and they left the Panda Palace.

"By the way, what were those black slimy things on my chicken?" Josh asked as they walked along Broadway.

"Seaweed," Dink said.

"No way!"

"Donny is right," Uncle Warren said. "But seaweed is good for you!"

"Good for fish, maybe," Josh said.

It started to rain, so they walked quickly. At the apartment, Roger handed them their backpacks. "How was dinner?" he asked.

"I ate black seaweed," Josh muttered.

Roger grinned. "Good stuff, isn't it?" he asked.

Uncle Warren and the kids rode the elevator to the tenth floor, then walked down the hall to a gray door.

"Welcome to my little apartment," Uncle Warren said, and led them inside.

Uncle Warren's living room was filled with old, comfortable-looking furniture. The carpet on the floor was thick and soft. Paintings hung on the white walls between overflowing bookcases.

"Neat place, Uncle Warren," Dink said.

"Thank you, Donny. Ruth Rose, you get the guest room," Uncle Warren said. "You two boys can share the fold-out sofa here in the living room."

When they were all in their pajamas, they gathered around the dining room table to open their fortune cookies.

"The oldest gets to read his first," Uncle Warren said, cracking open his cookie.

He read his fortune silently, then laughed out loud. "Mine already came true. It says that I will meet nice people today, and I have!"

"Me next!" Josh said. He broke open his cookie and pulled out the thin paper. He read out loud: " 'Strange foods will please you.' "

Josh made a face. "I already ate seaweed," he said. "I can't wait to see what's next!"

"My turn," Ruth Rose said. She ate her cookie and looked at the fortune inside. "Oh, boy. This says I'll find treasure in unexpected places!"

"Your turn, nephew," Dink's uncle said. "Then it's to bed for all of us. We have a busy day tomorrow."

Dink cracked open his cookie and read his fortune to himself. "I don't get it," he said.

"Out loud, Dink!" Josh said.

美洲豹宝石

Dink read: " 'Your eyes will play tricks on you.' "

His uncle smiled. "Right now, your eyes look pretty sleepy, nephew. Off to slumberland!"

After breakfast the next morning, Uncle Warren and the kids walked back to the museum. It was still raining, so they huddled under two umbrellas.

They left the dripping umbrellas on the small landing at the top of the stairs. Another wet umbrella already stood in the umbrella stand. Uncle Warren opened the door, and they walked into his office.

A man greeted them just inside the door.

"Ah, James, you're here," Dink's uncle said. "Kids, this is James Pride, my assistant. James, this is my nephew, Donny Duncan, and his friends, Josh and Ruth Rose."

James Pride smiled at the kids. "Has Warren taken you sightseeing?" he asked.

"Not yet," Uncle Warren said. "But I've promised them a buggy ride through Central Park when the rain stops!"

James tapped the wooden crate. "I'll leave this to

you, Warren," he said. "My daughter loved the zoo, but now I'm behind on paperwork." He walked into his office and closed the door.

Just then, there was a knock on the outer office door. Uncle Warren opened it to a man in a wet raincoat.

"I'm Dr. Jeremy Pitts," the man said. "I believe Mr. Duncan is expecting me."

"Indeed I am, Dr. Pitts!" Dink's uncle said. He shook the man's hand. "Come in and dry off. Care for some tea?"

"No, thank you, I had breakfast at my hotel," Dr. Pitts said. He glanced around the office, then walked over to the large crate. "I see the treasures have arrived."

"Yes, the box came yesterday," Dink's uncle said. "Hang up your wet things and we'll get to work."

Once more, Uncle Warren pried off the crate's lid. He lifted each piece from the crate and handed it to Dr. Pitts, who carefully removed the wrappings. Using a special magnifying glass, he examined each item, then checked it off a list.

The kids helped by re-wrapping the treasures. There were several more gold cups, a few carved animals, some pottery, and colorful masks made of jade and feathers.

"This all looks in fine condition," Dr. Pitts said. He glanced at his list. "But where is the jaguar, Mr. Duncan?"

Dink's uncle reached down into the crate. "Donny, can you give me a hand?" he asked.

Dink hurried over, and together they lifted the long, heavy package out of the crate.

"Place it here, please," Dr. Pitts said. He stood near the right side of Uncle Warren's desk.

"Watch the fish tank, Donny," Dink's uncle said as

they set the heavy package down on the desk.

They all gathered around as Dr. Pitts stripped away the brown paper. Josh let out a gasp as the plastic bubble wrap was removed.

The jaguar was solid gold. It was lying down, staring out of ruby eyes. Between its front paws was an emerald the size of a golf ball. The green jewel blazed under the office lights.

"Isn't it spectacular, kids?" Uncle Warren asked. "What workmanship!"

美洲豹宝石

Dr. Pitts wiped his hands on a handkerchief. Then he stroked the golden cat, feeling each curve and muscle.

"What's this?" he said suddenly, bending over the jewel.

"Something wrong?" Dink's uncle said.

Dr. Pitts peered through his magnifying glass at the jewel.

A minute later, he raised his head and looked at Dink's uncle. "Sir, this stone is a fake!"

Chapter 4

"What do you mean?" Dink's uncle asked. "I don't see how it could be fake."

Dr. Pitts rested a finger on the jewel. "This is not the original emerald," he explained. "In fact, it is not an emerald at all."

"But how could that be?" Dink's uncle cried.

"Look. I will show you," Dr. Pitts said. He took a small flashlight from his pocket.

"Will you please pull the shades and turn off the

美洲豹宝石

lights?" he asked.

Dink was closest to the windows, so he pulled the shades down and clicked off the light over the fish tank. Josh hurried over to the switches on the wall.

When the room was dark, Dr. Pitts turned on his flashlight and shone the beam on the jewel.

Suddenly, the flashlight went out. Dink heard something hit the desktop, then roll off and make a soft thud on the carpet.

"Sorry," Dr. Pitts muttered. "I seem to have dropped my flashlight. Can someone please…"

"I'll get it!" Josh said in the dark. He knelt down and fumbled around under the desk. "Found it," he said a moment later. He stood, switched it on, and aimed the light at the desk.

"Thank you, young man," Dr. Pitts said. He took the flashlight and pointed it at the jewel once more.

"You see, if this were a real emerald, the light would penetrate," he explained. "The light beam would go to the heart of the jewel."

He tapped a finger against the jewel. "But this is just glass. Notice how the light bounces off the

115

surface. The light does not enter the stone."

He shone the light on his own face.

"Of course, that is just my opinion. You are welcome to get another, Mr. Duncan."

"I certainly will!" Dink's uncle said.

He walked over to the wall and switched on the lights.

Dink blinked at the sudden brightness. His uncle looked very upset.

"But I simply can't understand how the real emerald could have been switched for a fake one!" Dink's uncle continued. "Are you absolutely sure?"

Dr. Pitts nodded: "Unfortunately, yes. I am sure."

"Then the swap must have taken place before the crate arrived," Uncle Warren declared. "Perhaps it happened in South America, when the jaguar was wrapped."

Dr. Pitts shook his head. "I'm sorry, but I was there for the packing. I assure you, when the jaguar was put into this crate, the emerald was real."

Dink's uncle stared at the jaguar. "I just don't see how it was possible!" he repeated.

Dr. Pitts shrugged. "Of course, I will have to report this to the police," he said. "If you want that second opinion…"

Dink's uncle hurried across the room and opened the door to James Pride's office. "James, please call Empire Jewelry on Broadway. Ask Regina Wu to come immediately. Tell her it's urgent!"

While they waited, Dr. Pitts examined the lock on the office door, then wrote something on a small pad.

Uncle Warren slumped in his chair and stared at the statue.

The kids sat on the rug and waited. Dink wanted to say something to his uncle, but he looked too upset.

Long minutes passed, then a knock sounded at the door. Uncle Warren jumped up. He let in a tall woman wearing a black raincoat. "Warren, I came as fast as I could," she said. "The streets are a mess!"

They shook hands, and Dink's uncle explained about the jaguar's jewel. "Dr. Pitts claims it's a fake!"

"May I?" Using a jeweler's magnifying glass, Ms. Wu examined the stone for a few minutes.

Then she removed a small bottle from her pocket and squeezed a drop of liquid onto the jewel. When the liquid dried, she wiped the stone with a cloth.

She shook her head. "He's right," she said. "This is a glass replica."

Uncle Warren fell back into his chair. "I am simply dumbfounded! Where did the switch take place? How? Who could possibly…"

"Pardon me," Dr. Pitts said. "The lock on the door does not appear to have been forced. Who besides you has a key to this office?"

"Mr. James Pride, my assistant, for one," Dink's uncle said. "And my friend Jean-Paul. He owns the restaurant next door to the museum. He let the deliveryman into my office yesterday."

"So this Jean-Paul has a key?" Dr. Pitts asked.

Uncle Warren shook his head. "Not to keep. I lent him my key, since the crate was due while James and I were away from the museum."

"So two people besides yourself had access to the jaguar, is that right?" Dr. Pitts asked. "Your assistant and your friend?"

"That is correct, but I assure you, neither of them has touched that statue. The idea is absurd!"

"Um, excuse me, Uncle Warren?" Dink said.

Everyone turned to look at Dink.

"Wouldn't there be fingerprints? I mean, if someone did take the real jewel, they'd leave prints on the fake one, right?"

No one spoke for a minute. Then Dr. Pitts smiled at Dink. "That's an excellent idea," he said. "And I think we should ask the police to look for fingerprints. They will, of course, find mine. But unless I miss my guess, no others."

"Why do you say that?" Ruth Rose asked.

"Because, young lady," Dr. Pitts said, "this thief was very clever. And clever thieves wear gloves."

Uncle Warren nodded at the phone. "Please call the police," he told Dr. Pitts. "They will prove that Jean-Paul and James are innocent!"

Dr. Pitts looked at Dink's uncle. "Excuse me, sir, but there is another suspect."

"And who would that be?" Uncle Warren asked.

"Yourself," Dr. Pitts said quietly.

Chapter 5

Dink heard thumping footsteps on the stairs just before two police officers entered the office. They listened to the story, then "invited" Dink's uncle down to the police station to answer more questions.

"Mr. Duncan, will you ask Mr. Pride and Jean-Paul to come with us?" one of the officers asked:

"I will," Dink's uncle said. "But believe me, this is a horrible mistake!"

美洲豹宝石

The officer nodded, pointing to the statue. "We'll have to take this, too. We'll check it for prints at the station."

"What about us?" Regina Wu asked. "Are Dr. Pitts and I free to go?"

"I have your addresses," the officer said. "We know where to find you."

"Of course," Dr. Pitts said. He and Regina Wu left.

Uncle Warren walked over to Dink. "Don't worry, nephew, this shouldn't take long," he said. "Stay with Yvonne until I get back."

When he bent down to hug Dink, he whispered, "Donny, remember your cookie!"

James Pride locked the office, and they all walked down the stairs. The two officers carried the rewrapped jaguar.

Jean-Paul hugged Yvonne, then joined Uncle Warren and James Pride in one of the police cruisers.

Dink, Josh, Ruth Rose, and Yvonne watched them drive away in the rain.

"Come inside," Yvonne said. "I will make something warm to drink. The men will be back in a jiffy, yes?"

She fixed the kids big mugs of hot chocolate. They sat at the window and watched the rain fall.

"Try not to worry," Yvonne said. "When the men return, then we solve the mystery, yes?"

She left the kids and passed through a blue curtain into the restaurant's kitchen.

"This is so weird!" Josh said.

"It stinks," Dink said. "I know my uncle wouldn't steal some dumb jewel!"

"But what happened to it?" Ruth Rose said. "Someone stole the real one!"

The kids sipped their hot chocolate and looked through the rain-streaked glass.

Dink stood up. "I wonder where the bathroom is?"

"Ask Yvonne," Ruth Rose said. "I think she's in the kitchen."

Josh slurped up the last of his drink. "And see if she has any more hot chocolate!" he said.

Dink walked toward the back of the restaurant. He passed through the blue curtain into the kitchen.

A pile of chopped broccoli sat on the counter next to a bowl of peeled raw onions. He looked around, but Yvonne wasn't there.

He saw another blue curtain, so he peeked through it, looking for the bathroom.

Just then, he heard a noise. Dink turned around and saw Yvonne slip through a narrow door. When the door closed behind her, it disappeared!

Dink blinked his eyes. The door was gone! There was no frame, no knob, and no hinges. He shook his head. Was he seeing things?

Dink found the bathroom, used it, then hurried back to Josh and Ruth Rose.

"Guys, listen to this!" Dink told them about Yvonne and the vanishing door. "After she shut the door, it disappeared, honest!"

"Disappearing doors?" Josh scoffed.

"Maybe it's her private bathroom or something," Ruth Rose said.

Suddenly, Dink remembered what his uncle had said to him. "When my uncle hugged me upstairs, he whispered, 'Remember your cookie' in my ear."

Josh grinned. "Maybe he was hungry," he said.

"Or maybe he was telling you to remember the fortune in your cookie!" Ruth Rose said.

"I saved it!" Dink said. He reached into his jacket pocket.

"What…?" Dink pulled out his uncle's brass key ring. "Where'd this come from?"

"That looks like the key to your uncle's office," Josh said.

"You're right!" Dink said. "He must have dropped it into my pocket when he hugged me!"

Dink reached back into his pocket and pulled out the slip of paper from his fortune cookie.

" 'Your eyes will play tricks on you,' " he read.

"Your fortune is already coming true!" Ruth Rose said. "I wonder if mine will. I'm supposed to find a treasure."

"Look!" said Josh suddenly. He pointed out the window. "There's that jewelry lady!"

Regina Wu hurried past the restaurant. The kids watched her slip inside the green door that led up to Uncle Warren's office.

美洲豹宝石

"Why is she going back up there?" Dink asked.

Just then, Yvonne came through the blue curtain. She was carrying a pitcher and a plate of cookies.

"More hot chocolate?" she asked. "And some of my special cranberry cookies!"

While Josh and Ruth Rose reached for the cookies, Dink stared out the window at the green door.

Suddenly, the door opened, and Regina Wu

stepped back outside. She closed the door behind her, then hurried away from the building.

Dink watched her dash up the street, raising her umbrella.

He stared after Regina Wu. What's going on? he wondered. Why would she go up to the office when she knows my uncle isn't there?

Suddenly, another thought struck him. Unless she went up to the office because he isn't there!

Chapter 6

Dink waited until Yvonne went back to the kitchen, then told the others what he'd just seen.

"But the office is locked," Josh said.

"Maybe she has a key," said Dink.

"Where would she get a key?" Josh asked. "You have one, and James Pride has the other."

"The question is," Ruth Rose said, "why did she go up there now, when nobody's around?"

Dink stood up. "We need to find out," he said. "Maybe she left a clue! Let's go before Yvonne gets back."

The kids hurried out into the rain. They scooted next door and slipped through the green door.

"Look," Dink said, pointing at the carpet. "Wet footprints!"

They hurried up the stairs. At the top, they saw more wet spots.

Dink's hand was shaking so badly he could barely unlock the door. The office was dark except for the light over the fish tank. The only sound was the tank's bubbling filter.

"This place is creepy," Josh whispered.

Dink checked the floor. "No wet footprints in here," he said quietly.

"Maybe Regina Wu wiped her feet before she came in," Ruth Rose whispered back.

"Maybe," Josh said. "But why are we whispering?" He flipped up the wall switches, and the lights, ceiling fan, and music all came on.

Dink squinted in the sudden brightness. "Okay,"

he said, "let's look around."

"For what?" Josh asked.

"I'm not sure," Dink answered. "But Regina Wu came up here for some reason. Either she took something or she left something behind."

"I'll go through the stuff in the crate," Ruth Rose said. "Dink, why don't you check out James's office? Josh, you take the trash can."

"Why do I have to go poking through the trash?" Josh asked.

"Because you're a good detective, and good detectives always check the trash," Ruth Rose said.

"Cool!" Josh said. He headed for the trash can next to the desk.

Dink walked into Mr. Pride's office. There was a small desk with locked drawers. A framed picture of three people stood on the desk. Dink recognized James Pride. The woman and child must be his wife and daughter, he thought.

Dink checked a gray file cabinet in one corner. It was locked. Then he ran his fingers across the bookshelves. He checked inside some of the books, not knowing what he was looking for. He even peeked under the rug. He couldn't tell if anything was missing, and he found no clues.

As he started to leave, Dink suddenly noticed that one wall seemed different from the others. He stared at it, trying to figure out what looked odd about it.

Then he realized what it was:this wall had no bookshelves, no file cabinets, no pictures, no anything! It was completely bare.

美洲豹宝石

Dink stepped closer and ran his fingers over the striped wallpaper. Just above his head, he felt a thin crack. He followed the crack with his fingers until he felt another crack, this one running down toward the floor. Two feet in the opposite direction, a third crack ran to the floor. The cracks were almost hidden in the wallpaper.

Dink jumped back as if his hand had been burned. "Guys!" he shouted.

Josh and Ruth Rose came running into James's office.

Dink showed them his discovery. "I think it's a secret door!" he said.

He tried to force his fingers into the cracks, but the door wouldn't budge.

"If there were stairs behind this wall," Ruth Rose said, "they would lead right to the secret door in Yvonne's kitchen!"

Josh's eyes opened wide. "That would mean she could get in here without a key!"

"Do you think she was coming here when I saw her downstairs?" Dink asked.

"Maybe she met Regina Wu!" Ruth Rose said. "Yvonne could have let her in."

"Maybe," Dink said, walking back to his uncle's office. "But why? We gotta keep looking. Did you find anything in the trash, Josh?"

"Zilch," Josh said.

On the floor where Ruth Rose had been sitting was a pile of packing peanuts. She had unwrapped each artifact, then put it aside.

"All I found was the same treasures we looked at yesterday," she said. "I don't think anything is missing."

The kids continued to search. Behind curtains. Under the Oriental rug. They pulled out everything from every desk drawer. They even dug in the dirt in the potted plants next to the windows.

"Nothing but a secret door that doesn't open," Josh muttered.

"And we can't check out the door downstairs with Yvonne in the kitchen," Ruth Rose said.

"So now what?" Josh asked.

"I don't know," Dink said. He looked at Josh and Ruth Rose. "But my uncle is counting on us to find something up here, and I'm not gonna stop till I find it!"

Chapter 7

"But we've already looked at everything," Josh said, flopping down on the rug.

Ruth Rose walked over to the fish tank and picked up the container of food.

"That's weird," she said. "There are already some flakes floating on the water. Did one of you guys feed the fish?"

"I didn't," Dink said.

"Me neither," said Josh.

美洲豹宝石

Ruth Rose looked at the food floating on the top. "Well, someone did."

"Maybe it was the fish fairy," Josh said.

"OH MY GOSH!" Ruth Rose screamed.

"What's the matter?" Dink asked. Josh jumped to his feet, and he and Dink hurried over.

"Look what's on the bottom!" Ruth Rose said. She pointed down through the water.

Josh put his nose up against the glass. "Looks like a bunch of rocks to me," he said.

Ruth Rose frowned. "Somebody go turn out the lights," she said.

Josh gave Dink a push. "Go ahead, Dinkus!"

Dink hurried over to the wall and flipped down the switches. The music, fan, and lights all went off.

Ruth Rose pointed at the bottom of the tank. "See that glowy green rock? I think it's the jewel!"

Dink elbowed Josh aside and looked at the stone. "No, it's too big," he said. "The emerald was like a golf ball, remember?"

"Things always look bigger underwater," Ruth Rose said. "Your eyes are playing tricks on you again, Dink!"

Ruth Rose reached down and plucked the green rock out of the tank. Water dripped onto the floor as she wiped it on her jeans.

Out of the water, the rock didn't look anything like the other rocks in the fish tank. In the tank light, the rock shone a lustrous green.

"Wow!" Dink said. "It's beautiful!"

"How did it get in there?" Josh asked.

"I guess the thief dumped it in," Dink answered.

"But why would the thief do that?" Josh asked.

Ruth Rose shook her head. "Maybe he needed a quick place to hide it."

美洲豹宝石

Dink nodded. "James was here early this morning. Maybe we caught him in the act!"

"I'm turning on the lights," Josh said. He headed for the wall switches.

"Stop!" Dink said suddenly. "What's that sound?"

"What sound?" Josh asked as he turned on the fan, music, and lights.

Dink walked over and flipped the switches down again. "Now listen," he whispered in the darkness. "Hear it?"

"I think I do," Ruth Rose said. "Like a little buzzing."

"Maybe it's the fish tank," Josh said.

Ruth Rose clicked off the bubbler. "Nope, I still hear it," she said.

"Now I hear it, too," Josh said. "What can it be? Everything's turned off!"

"I'm going to turn on just the lights," Dink said.

When they could see, the kids began prowling around the office.

Dink stopped in front of the bookcase. "Guys, it's louder over here!"

Josh giggled. "The Case of the Buzzing Books!" he said.

Dink stood on tiptoe and ran his hands over the shelves. He felt a small button and pushed it. Suddenly, a shelf slid open. "Look!" he cried.

"Hey! Those books are fake!" Josh said. "It's a hidden compartment!"

The space behind the fake books held a small TV set and VCR. With the compartment open, the buzzing was louder. Then the VCR clicked, and the noise stopped.

"It was rewinding," Josh said. "It must have come to the end of the tape. My dad's machine does the same thing."

"Yeah, but rewinding what?" Dink asked.

Then the VCR clicked again. The kids watched as a red light came on and the numbers on the machine's face started counting up—01, 02, 03…

"Hey!" Josh said. "Now it's recording!"

"Maybe your uncle has it for security," Ruth Rose said.

"You could be right, Ruth Rose," Dink said.

He glanced at the ceiling. "There must be a camera somewhere in the office."

"Do you think we're on a video?" Ruth Rose said. "Let's take a peek!"

"Good idea!" said Josh.

Dink quickly rewound the tape to the beginning, then turned on the TV and hit "play" on the VCR.

An image came on the screen. For a moment, the tape showed them standing in front of the TV and VCR.

"Cool!" Josh said.

Then the picture jumped and changed. Now the office looked empty and dark. They watched as the office door opened and James Pride walked in.

"This must be earlier today," Ruth Rose said. "James got here before us."

"Maybe it recorded him stealing the jewel!" Josh said.

They watched James walk over and switch on the lights. Then he took off his raincoat and walked into his own office.

The kids looked at each other. James hadn't gone

anywhere near the crate.

"Hit 'fast forward'," Josh said. "We can scan ahead."

Dink pushed the button, and the tape began whirring fast. The picture on the screen flickered.

"Look!" Ruth Rose said. "Something's happening!"

Dink quickly pressed "play." The tape slowed, and the kids saw themselves and Uncle Warren walk into the office.

They watched as they met James Pride. Then Uncle Warren let in Dr. Pitts. The crate was opened again, and Dr. Pitts checked the contents of each package.

"Now we take the jaguar out of the crate," Dink said.

"And the doc tells us it's a fake," Josh added.

Ruth Rose pointed at the screen. "And here he takes out his flashlight."

"And Dink and I pull the shades and shut off the lights," Josh said.

The picture went black.

The next thing they saw was the light from Dr.

美洲豹宝石

Pitts's flashlight. Then it went out.

"This is when you found the flashlight for him," Ruth Rose told Josh.

A minute later, Dr. Pitts had the light in his hand again and was shining it on the jaguar's jewel.

Then the lights came back on. Regina Wu soon showed up, and then the police came. The tape showed everyone leaving the office.

Dink reached out to hit the "stop" button.

"Wait!" Ruth Rose said. "What about Yvonne and Regina Wu?"

"Oh, yeah," said Dink. "Good thinking, Ruth Rose."

They watched the empty office for a while. Dink was about to scan ahead when the door to James Pride's office opened and Yvonne walked in!

"The secret door does connect to Yvonne's kitchen!" Ruth Rose said.

They watched as Yvonne walked across the office—straight toward the fish tank! When she got there, Yvonne made kissing noises at the fish. Then she picked up the fish food, sprinkled some into the tank, and turned around and left.

The kids looked at each other. "I guess she's not the thief," said Josh.

Ruth Rose turned back to the TV. "What about Regina Wu?" she asked.

They watched the tape for a few more minutes, but Regina Wu never appeared. Eventually, they saw themselves come through the office door.

Dink stopped the tape and hit the "rewind" button.

"I wonder why your uncle didn't tell the police about this tape?" Josh said. "If they watched it, they'd at least know that James and Yvonne didn't steal the jewel."

Dink nodded. "Yvonne didn't know the jewel was in the fish tank," he said, "so I'll bet Jean-Paul didn't put it there."

Dink looked sad. "And if Regina Wu couldn't even get in the office…"

Ruth Rose let out a gasp. "That means— "

"That means my uncle is the only other suspect," Dink said.

Chapter 8

Josh's mouth fell open. "Your uncle's the thief?" he asked.

"Josh!" Ruth Rose scolded. She turned to Dink. "Your uncle isn't the thief," she said. "He never had a chance to take the jewel. We were with him when he opened the crate, and he sure didn't take it on the tape we just saw."

Dink felt sick even thinking that his uncle might

have stolen the emerald. "What about when we turned out all the lights?" he asked.

"But that was so quick," Ruth Rose said. "I don't see how he—"

"Guys! The desk!" Josh said suddenly. "Look at it! Do you see anything different?"

Dink and Ruth Rose looked at Uncle Warren's desk.

"What do you mean?" Dink asked. "There's nothing but the blotter and the letter opener, the same as yesterday and this morning."

Josh hit the "play" button on the VCR. He fast-forwarded until the tape showed the room and everyone in it.

"There!" he shouted a moment later. "Look at the letter opener. The tip is pointing toward the windows, right?"

"Yeah, so what?" Dink said.

"Wait a sec and you'll see."

In the film, the lights went out. After Dr. Pitts finished shining his flashlight on the jewel, the lights came back on.

"Now look!" Josh cried. "See, the letter opener is pointing away from the windows. It got turned around!"

"Why does it matter, Josh?" Ruth Rose asked.

"I don't know," Josh said. "But someone picked up the letter opener while the lights were out, then put it down again."

"Who was standing closest to it?" Dink asked, hitting "stop" and "rewind."

"I think Dr. Pitts was," Josh said. "He was standing right in front of the jaguar. The letter opener was a few inches away."

"But why would he want the letter opener in the dark?" Ruth Rose asked.

Just then, they heard thumps outside the office door, like someone stomping on a carpet.

"Who's that?" Ruth Rose whispered.

Josh gulped. "Is the door locked?"

"I don't think so!" Dink whispered back. He swept a hand over the wall switches. The room darkened except for the small light over the fish tank.

"Look!" Josh whispered. Through the frosted-

A to Z 神秘案件

glass window in the door, the kids saw a tall shadow.

They heard a click, and the doorknob turned.

"Hide!" Dink whispered. "James's office!"

The kids dashed into the small office. Dink left the door open a crack so he could see who entered.

It was Dr. Pitts.

Chapter 9

Dr. Pitts stepped into the dark office. The kids watched him creep toward Uncle Warren's desk.

Suddenly, he switched on his flashlight. Turning slowly, Dr. Pitts played the beam around the room.

In James's office, Dink shrank back against the wall. He held his breath. Next to him, he could feel Josh and Ruth Rose trembling.

Dink dared to peek out again. The flashlight was

now lying on the desk. Its beam made a yellow circle on the fish tank.

Dr. Pitts was crouched down, staring into the tank.

Suddenly, he swore. Dink watched Dr. Pitts grab his flashlight and shine it wildly around the room.

Dink froze and held his breath. When he peeked out again, Dr. Pitts was shining the flashlight beam at the floor, near his feet.

He bent over and touched something on the floor.

Dink thought about the water Ruth Rose had dripped there.

Dr. Pitts once more shone the flashlight's beam around the dark office. The light fell on James's door.

"Who's in there?" Dr. Pitts said.

Dink closed his eyes. He felt his whole body grow cold. Ruth Rose let out a soft gasp.

Then Dink heard footsteps. Dr. Pitts was coming toward their hiding spot!

We have to get out of here! Dink thought. He pressed himself against the wall—but suddenly the wall wasn't there!

美洲豹宝石

Dink felt a strong hand grab his arm. Another hand went over his mouth. Struggling, Dink felt himself being dragged backward.

"Don't speak!" a hoarse voice whispered in his ear. "Come with me!"

Too frightened to resist, Dink let himself be led. He reached out for Josh and Ruth Rose but felt nothing. Where were they?

"Down here, quickly!" the voice said.

Dink felt stairs under his feet. As he stumbled down, he smelled something familiar.

At the bottom of the stairs, a door opened. Dink saw light. He smelled onions.

He was in Yvonne's kitchen!

Then Josh and Ruth Rose piled into him. Yvonne released his arm and slammed the door shut. This was the same narrow door Dink had seen her close before.

"Come," Yvonne said, putting a finger to her lips.

Yvonne rushed them toward the front of the restaurant.

"The thief is still up there," she said. "I must lock

the outside door. He will be trapped, no?"

She hurried toward the exit, but Dr. Pitts was already racing past the restaurant's window.

"He is gone!" Yvonne wailed. "Now we will never catch him!"

"It's okay," Dink said, grinning. "I have a feeling we caught him on video."

"Video?" Yvonne asked. "I do not understand."

"My uncle has a hidden camera in the office," Dink explained.

He looked at Josh and Ruth Rose. "I hit the 'rewind' button before we had to hide, remember? I'll bet the tape rewound to the beginning and started recording again before Dr. Pitts came in."

"Not only that," Josh said. "His fingerprints should be on the letter opener!"

"Letter opener?" Yvonne asked, looking at the three kids.

"I think I've figured that out," Ruth Rose said. "When the lights were turned off, he must have used the letter opener to pry the jewel out of the jaguar's paws. Then he quickly switched in the fake and slipped the real jewel into the fish tank."

"But what does it matter, this camera and these fingerprints," Yvonne said, "if he has the jewel?"

"But he doesn't!" Ruth Rose said. She opened her fist and showed the emerald to Yvonne.

"It was in the fish tank, and I got it out before he did!"

"How lovely!" Yvonne said, giving Ruth Rose a hug.

"Now what?" Josh asked.

Yvonne went for the wall phone. "Now we call the police!" she said.

Chapter 10

Jean-Paul held up his water glass. "I propose a toast," he said.

Uncle Warren and Yvonne raised their glasses.

"To three brave and smart kids!" Jean-Paul said, looking at Dink, Josh, and Ruth Rose.

"Hear, hear," Uncle Warren said. "You put a crook behind bars and saved a priceless jewel from being stolen."

美洲豹宝石

"It all started with your telling me to remember my cookie," Dink told his uncle.

Dink's uncle smiled. "I knew if I gave you my key and reminded you not to trust what you saw, you'd figure it out."

"Ruth Rose's cookie said she'd find a treasure in an unexpected place," Josh said, "and she did!"

"And Josh noticed that the letter opener had been moved," Ruth Rose said.

"Yeah, and Dink found the video recorder behind the books," Josh said.

Dink smiled at Yvonne. "And thank goodness you rescued us!"

"When I came to give you more cookies, you were gone," Yvonne said. "Then I saw that doctor man sneaking into the downstairs door. I ran up the back stairs!"

"Why do you have those hidden doors?" Ruth Rose asked Dink's uncle.

"Many years ago, the Porter Museum was a private home," he explained. "Old Mr. and Mrs. Porter's servants used that back stairway to go up and down. When the Porter home became a museum, the architects decided to leave the doors and stairway as they were."

"I'm glad they did!" Josh said.

"When I'm away, Yvonne comes up to feed my fish," Uncle Warren said.

Yvonne smiled. "And you thought perhaps I was

the one who took the jewel, no?"

Dink blushed. "Yeah, but then I saw Regina Wu sneak into the building, so I thought it was her, too!"

Uncle Warren laughed. "She called a while ago and explained that," he said. "She'd forgotten her umbrella and went back up to get it."

"Uncle Warren," Dink said, "why didn't you tell

the police about the camera and the video?"

His uncle laughed. "I honestly forgot the camera was there!" he said. "Besides, I'm a dunce when it comes to anything electronic. James had it installed, but even he tends to forget about it."

"The part I don't understand is how Dr. Pitts could switch the glass emerald for the jewel so fast," Josh said. "And in the dark!"

"I'm sure he practiced," Uncle Warren said. "And when he first came in, he must have spotted the letter opener on my desk."

"So that's why he wanted us to put the jaguar down on the desk close to the fish tank," Dink said. "He knew he was going to slip the emerald into the water."

His uncle nodded. "Yes, and then come back later to get it."

"So when he told you to get a second opinion," Ruth Rose said, "the jewel really was a fake. Because he'd just taken the real one, right?"

"Right," Uncle Warren said. "And he almost got away with his scam."

He smiled at his dinner companions. "But he didn't figure on three detectives hiding in James's office!"

Just then, they heard bells jingling outside the restaurant.

"Aha, our ride is here!" Uncle Warren said, standing up.

"What ride?" Dink asked. "Can't we walk back to your apartment?"

"We're not going right back, nephew," his uncle said. "Come!"

He led everyone outside, where a large white horse stood waiting. The horse was harnessed to a buggy. All along the harness leather were small lights and bells.

A short man climbed down from the driver's seat. He wore a spiffy gray suit and a black top hat.

"Hello, I'm Alfie," the man said, "and this lovely horse is Prince."

"Climb aboard!" Uncle Warren said.

"Cool!" Josh said, hoisting himself into the buggy. "Where are we going?"

"Who cares?" Ruth Rose said, climbing in next to Josh.

Uncle Warren helped Dink up and then sat next to him.

"We are going to see New York City by night," he said. "I don't want you to go home thinking all we have here is loud traffic and jewel thieves!"

He tapped on the back of the buggy. "Take us away, Alfie!"

"Au revoir!" cried Yvonne and Jean-Paul from the sidewalk. "See you tomorrow!"

Alfie clicked his tongue at Prince, and the buggy

美洲豹宝石

began to move. Slowly, the horse clip-clopped down the street.

    Dink sat back and gazed up at the sky. A billion stars blazed down at him. One star was larger than the others, and it looked green, like a jewel.

The green star blinked, then disappeared.

Dink laughed.

"What's funny?" Josh asked.

Dink shook his head. "Nothing," he said. "Just my eyes playing tricks on me again."

Text copyright © 2000 by Ron Roy
Illustrations copyright © 2000 by John Steven Gurney
All rights reserved under International and Pan-American Copyright Conventions.
Published in the United States by Random House, Inc., New York,
and simultaneously in Canada by Random House of Canada Limited, Toronto.

本书中英双语版由中南博集天卷文化传媒有限公司与企鹅兰登（北京）文化发展有限公司合作出版。

"企鹅"及其相关标识是企鹅兰登已经注册或尚未注册的商标。
未经允许，不得擅用。
封底凡无企鹅防伪标识者均属未经授权之非法版本。

©中南博集天卷文化传媒有限公司。本书版权受法律保护。未经权利人许可，任何人不得以任何方式使用本书包括正文、插图、封面、版式等任何部分内容，违者将受到法律制裁。

著作权合同登记号：字18-2023-258

图书在版编目（CIP）数据

美洲豹宝石：汉英对照 /（美）罗恩·罗伊著；
（美）约翰·史蒂文·格尼绘；王芬芬译. -- 长沙：湖南少年儿童出版社，2024.10. --（A to Z神秘案件）.
ISBN 978-7-5562-7817-6

Ⅰ．H319.4
中国国家版本馆CIP数据核字第2024X9C293号

A TO Z SHENMI ANJIAN MEIZHOUBAO BAOSHI

A to Z神秘案件 美洲豹宝石

[美] 罗恩·罗伊 著　　[美] 约翰·史蒂文·格尼 绘　　王芬芬 译

责任编辑：唐 凌　李 炜	策划出品：李 炜　张苗苗　文赛峰
策划编辑：文赛峰	特约编辑：杜佳美
营销编辑：付 佳　杨 朔　周晓茜	封面设计：霍雨佳
版权支持：王媛媛	版式设计：马睿君
插图上色：河北传图文化	内文排版：马睿君

出 版 人：刘星保
出　　版：湖南少年儿童出版社
地　　址：湖南省长沙市晚报大道89号
邮　　编：410016
电　　话：0731-82196320
常年法律顾问：湖南崇民律师事务所　柳成柱律师
经　　销：新华书店

开　本：875 mm × 1230 mm　1/32	印　刷：三河市中晟雅豪印务有限公司
字　数：87千字	印　张：5.125
版　次：2024年10月第1版	印　次：2024年10月第1次印刷
书　号：ISBN 978-7-5562-7817-6	定　价：280.00元（全10册）

若有质量问题，请致电质量监督电话：010-59096394　团购电话：010-59320018